BRAVE GIRLS

Faithful Friends

Other books in the Brave Girls brand

BRAVE GIRLS
Faithful Friends

Written by
JENNIFER GERELDS

A Division of Thomas Nelson Publishers

NASHVILLE   MEXICO CITY   RIO DE JANEIRO

Published in Nashville, Tennessee, by Tommy Nelson. Tommy Nelson is an imprint of Thomas Nelson. Thomas Nelson is a registered trademark of HarperCollins Christian Publishing, Inc.

Tommy Nelson titles may be purchased in bulk for educational, business, fund-raising, or sales promotional use. For information, please e-mail SpecialMarkets@ThomasNelson.com.

Unless otherwise noted, Scripture quotations are taken from INTERNATIONAL CHILDREN'S BIBLE®. © 1986, 1988, 1999 by Thomas Nelson, Inc. All rights reserved.

Scripture quotations marked NKJV are taken from THE NEW KING JAMES VERSION. © 1982 by Thomas Nelson, Inc. Used by permission. All rights reserved.

Library of Congress Cataloging-in-Publication Data is on file.

Printed in the United States of America

15 16 17 18 19 20 RRD 6 5 4 3 2 1

Conten...

We must always thank God for you. And we should do this because it is right. It is right because your faith is growing more and more. And the love that every one of you has for each other is also growing.

2 Thessalonians 1:3

Hi! It's the Brave Girls here. We're so excited that you've picked up our book about friends. It has been a lot of fun to write about all the ways God has wired us differently but somehow brings us together in one big, happy family. Well, happy when we're loving each other the way God wants us to, that is. And we hope that's what you'll find in here: different ways we all can learn to find good friends and be one too.

Of course, I (Gracie) have had a lot of hands-on experience in the finding-friends department, ever since I had to move to this town from my home in Pennsylvania. Leaving my old friends and starting over seemed impossible. But it turned out to be a really good thing because I've met a new group of girls who know God really well. They've shared His love with me, and now . . . well, I've got a bunch of great new friends. But best of all is my new *best* friend—Jesus! I hope our book helps you discover God's forever friendship too!

Speaking of hope, I (Hope) just wanted to add that making

friends might seem uncomfortable at first, but it is so worth it in the end. I'm different from Gracie because I've lived here all my life. It would be easy to stick with the same friends. But if I had kept to myself, I never would've met Gracie! That's why we've put so many practical tips in here on how to make new friends and keep the ones you have. We want you to see God's love keep growing and growing, just like we have!

Sound good? Then read on, and get ready to watch God build you into the best friend ever—and turn your friendships into lasting treasures!

Love,

Hope Glory Faith
gracie Honor

GOD IS MY BEST FRIEND

> The LORD Himself will go before you. He will be with you. He will not leave you or forget you.
>
> Deuteronomy 31:8

Imagine for a moment the best kind of friend in the whole wide world. What would that person be like?

Certainly, she would love you all the time. She would know what makes you happy and look for ways to bring a smile to your face. When you are sad, she'd know just how to cheer you up. Most likely, she would like the things you like and think that you are super special. And if someone or something tried to hurt you, she would try her best to defend and protect you. Best of all, she would always be ready to talk, listen, and spend time with you whenever you needed it—today, tomorrow, and *forever*.

Do you have a friend like that?

If you trust in Jesus, you do! Jesus is the very best friend you could ever have. He loves you more than anybody on earth. He knows everything about you, from your deepest feelings to your greatest dreams, and He thinks you're wonderful! He proved how much He cared when He gave up His life and rose again so you could be in God's family. Now He lives in heaven, eager to be your very best friend. Simply put, Jesus is crazy about you. Best of all, Jesus never changes, and His friendship is forever.

Prayer Pointer

Jesus, I am amazed that You care so much about me. Help me grow closer to You each day.

I pray that [the Lord] will give you
a spirit that will make you wise
in the knowledge of God.

Ephesians 1:17

D id you know that water comes in three different forms? If you
think you know what they are, circle the right answers below:

rivers   oceans   vapor   jelly   liquid
candy   fire   solid   soda   rain

If you picked vapor (like steam), liquid (like rain), and solid (like ice), you're right! Isn't it weird that water can look and act so differently, depending on the situation? But no matter its form, one thing is for sure: it's still water!

If you think about it, water helps us know how God can live and work as three different persons—the Father, the Son, and the Holy Spirit—but still be just one God. All three persons of God, also called the Trinity, work, love, and serve each other perfectly. When you join God's family by trusting Jesus to be your Savior, you get to be a part of that beautiful friendship. Now you have a heavenly Daddy (God the Father), a Savior and Friend (God the Son), and a Helper who lives inside you to lead you closer to God (God the Holy Spirit). You are completely surrounded by God's love, inside and out!

Prayer Pointer

God, thank You for being everything I
need. I love being in Your family!

The LORD sees the good people. He listens to their prayers. . . . The LORD hears good people when they cry out to Him. He saves them from all their troubles.

Psalm 34:15, 17

Do you remember the first time you ever met your best friend? Chances are the first conversation was a bit awkward. But the more you two talked, the more you found in common with each other. And now you're as comfortable with your best friend as you are with anyone in your family.

The same is true when you are hanging out with God. At first, it might seem really weird to talk to someone you can't see. Many kids *and* adults wonder, *What should I say?* or *How does this work?* and *What if I mess up?*

But relax! God is super interested in whatever you have to say. You will be surprised how quickly you become comfortable telling Him whatever's on your mind. Soon, you'll be talking out loud or in your heart all day long and including your new best friend in everything you do.

So what are you waiting for? Here are a few icebreakers just to get the conversation going:

Praise: "God, You are so _____ (fill in with words that describe who He is, such as *powerful*, *forgiving*, *faithful*, or *kind*)."

Confess: "Lord, I admit that I have _____
(name your thoughts, attitudes, or actions that go against
God's directions in the Bible). Please forgive me. Thank
You that You always forgive me!"

Thank: "Jesus, thank You for _____
(name the good things you have in your life). Everything I
have comes from You!"

Ask: "Lord, You are all powerful and good. Would You please
help me _____? Also, would you please help _____
(my family, friends, the poor, the missionaries, our leaders,
etc.) who need_____?"

Prayer Pointer

God, thank You for always listening to what I say.
Help me always come to You with my thoughts.

> The LORD said to me, "Human being, believe all the words that I will speak to you. And listen carefully."
>
> Ezekiel 3:10

How well do you know your best friend? Take this simple quiz to find out:

1. Her favorite color is _____ .
2. Her favorite activity is _____ .
3. What always makes her laugh is _____ .

Now talk to her, and ask her these same questions. How well did you do?

The truth is we get to know other people by just being around them. We watch them and learn what they do. Most importantly, we listen to what they say. When we do, we can learn all kinds of information that helps us understand who they really are and how to be a closer friend.

The same is totally true about God. We get to talk to Him through prayer, and He talks to us through the Bible and the Holy Spirit, who lives inside us. The Bible is different from any other book because God Himself wrote it, using different people to record His exact words. Because the Bible comes from God, everything in it helps us understand how to be friends with Him. The Holy Spirit helps us remember and follow what God tells us in His Word.

Prayer Pointer

Jesus, help me grow closer to God by
listening and obeying God's Word.

Every good action and every
perfect gift is from God.

James 1:17

H ave you ever played with an optical illusion? You might have been flipping through a book and found a page full of rect-angles—or so it seemed. But if you look hard enough, your eyes will adjust to actually see . . . a dog! Pretty cool, right?

Some people, no matter how hard they look at the image, only see strange black rectangles. But others, after their eyes have adjusted, suddenly see something else: the name *Jesus*!

The same is true in life. Many people think God can't be seen. They go through each day as if they have to solve all their problems on their own. Good and bad things happen, and they assume it is all happening by chance or luck. They can't see God's hand in it.

But God has given His children special eyes to see the picture of life more clearly. Jesus is always there, and we are never alone! Though we can't see Jesus with our eyes, His Spirit is inside of us, and our heavenly Father watches over us and guides our every step. And God promises to work out everything that happens for our good.

So when you wake up this morning, don't miss the bigger picture. Celebrate every bird that sings, every tasty bite you eat, and every hug from family and friends as proof that God loves to love you!

— Prayer Pointer —

Father, give me eyes to see all the ways
You love and care for me.

Be wise in the way you act with people
who are not believers. . . . When you talk,
you should always be kind and wise.

Colossians 4:5-6

So your mom made her yummiest chocolate-chip cookies last night, and you brought some to school. You were so excited because you couldn't wait to pass them around to your friends at lunch! They didn't even have to ask for a cookie because your friends know that you always share good things with them.

Now think about Jesus for a minute. He is good, right? Like, *really* good. Better than chocolate-chip cookies. Better than a new video game or a sport or a vacation or any of the other things we love to show and tell our friends all about. So if we know that being friends with Jesus means love, joy, and everlasting peace with God, why don't we share the Good News with our friends who don't know Him?

We have to admit it: we are afraid that our friends might not like what we say about God or think we are weird. But Jesus wants us to share what we know because it gives others a taste of God's goodness—just like the sweetness in that cookie. When your friends are ready, they will be so glad you were willing to share the sweet treat of knowing Jesus.

Prayer Pointer

Jesus, make me brave to share Your
love and truth with my friends.

Choosing Friends

Jesus said, "Come follow me."

Matthew 4:19

How easy is it for you to make friends? Using the scale below, with 1 being the most difficult thing in the world and 10 being easy as microwaved popcorn, circle the number that best describes your friend-making skill level:

1   2   3   4   5   6   7   8   9   10

Did you rate yourself high or low? Even for the most outgoing kid, making new friends can be challenging. But Jesus gives us a great tip. When He was seeking out the twelve men who would become His closest friends and followers, He prayed! During an all-night prayer session, God the Son asked God the Father to lead Him to the right people. Then Jesus obeyed and invited each man to be His follower.

Since we aren't Jesus, it would be really weird if we asked someone to be our follower. But we can ask God to help us find the right people who will make good friends. Then, as we go through our day, we can look for signs of good friend material like kindness, respectfulness, and a love for God. When we see those good qualities in others, we need to be bold like Jesus and strike up a conversation with them. God has a cool way of bringing His people together!

Prayer Pointer

Lord, please help me find good friends who love You too.

WHEN a good maN pRays,
gReat tHiNgs HappeN.

James 5:16

Have you ever had a friend come to you with a problem too big for you to handle? Maybe her parents were getting divorced or his family member was really sick. You wanted to be able to help your friend in some way, but you knew you didn't have the power to do anything about it.

But actually, you have far more power than you know. Remember, the God who spoke a word to create an entire universe loves *you* and lives in you. He welcomes you to come anytime before His grand throne room in heaven to talk about anything and everything you need. And He, in His great wisdom, knows exactly the right way to respond and has all the power to fix the problem!

One way to pray boldly and regularly for family and friends is by making a power box. No worries, no electricity is necessary. You just need the mighty power of God. Here's what to do:

- Ask your parents to help you find a plastic recipe box and some 3 x 5 index cards. (Both can be found at most dollar stores.)
- Write the name of the person you want to pray for at the top of the card.
- Pick two or three Bible verses that would meet the need of that friend. (For example, if you know she worries

about not having clothes as nice as everyone else's, you can find a verse about contentment or about how God clothes us with everlasting beauty.)

- Below the verses, record specific prayer requests. Just make short statements that will help you remember what to pray for.
- On the other side of the card, record the way God answers your specific request and the date.
- Each day, open your power box and select one or two cards. And pray for your friends using the verses and reminders.

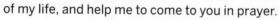

Prayer Pointer

Father, please help me to trust You with every part of my life, and help me to come to you in prayer.

If [a man] stumbles, He will not fall, because the LORD holds His hand.

Psalm 37:23-24

In your opinion, do you think roller coasters are awesome or awful? It seems crazy to step inside a metal car that shoots across a narrow track at insane angles and heights. So what is the attraction? The thrill!

The slow *chink-chink-chink* climb up the first ridge, the dizzying height, the sound of release when the bottom drops out and you feel your stomach in your throat. It's intense, and your heart races with the speed of the coaster! And even though you don't know what's coming next, you are smiling bigger than ever because it's super fun, and you know the coaster holding you will keep you on its track and eventually deliver you safely back to your destination.

Learning to trust God is a lot like stepping into the car of a roller coaster. It can feel scary to commit to following Him and give Him full control of your life. But God is holding you firmly through the twists and turns that life brings. When you realize every moment is under His control, you can rest, enjoy the ride, and lift up your hands in delight, knowing He will deliver you safely to your destination.

Prayer Pointer

God, thank You for being by my side. Please help me keep my life on track.

A friend loves you all the time.
Proverbs 17:17

Now that you know a little more about your *real* best friend forever, can you name a few ways God shows you that He wants to be your friend?

_____

_____

_____

_____

_____

_____

_____

_____

_____

_____

_____

_____

_____

_____

_____

BIBLE FRIENDS

The Blame Game

Confess your sins to each other and pray for each other. Do this so that God can heal you.

James 5:16

If anyone should have been best friends, it should have been Adam and Eve. Think about it: Eve had been formed right from Adam's side, so they were closely connected to each other and to God. Best of all, they lived in a perfect paradise where they walked and talked with God every day.

But sin has a really sad way of taking something beautiful and messing it all up. When Adam and Eve disobeyed God, they immediately turned on each other. Adam blamed Eve for the problem. Eve blamed the snake who tricked her (Genesis 2:21–3:13). But it didn't matter who started it. Both of them felt the pain of a broken friendship with each other and God. Sin always makes good relationships go very, very bad.

But God has fixed the problem through Jesus. When we trust and follow Jesus, we don't need to play the blame game anymore. We know we are sinners and so are our friends. Whenever we hurt one another, God helps us forgive. And God always answers! Each mended friendship gives us a taste of what it will be like in heaven, where all fighting and separation will end and love will win!

Prayer Pointer

Lord, I know I'm a sinner. Thanks for forgiving
me and helping me forgive others too.

He has shown you, O man, what is good;
and what does the Lord require of you
but to do justly, to love mercy, and
to walk humbly with your God?

Micah 6:8 NKJV

Have you ever taken a walk by yourself? How would walking that same route with a close friend be different?

When you're alone, you have only your own thoughts to entertain you. But walk with a friend, and a whole new world of conversation and ideas opens up. You're no longer taking in the scenes by yourself; you're sharing them with someone else. And as you walk and talk and connect through the fun and exercise, you find that spending time with your friend makes you closer to each other.

Enoch knew all about walking and talking with his best friend. He did it every day of his life. But Enoch's closest friend wasn't from school or even a family member. It was God! Enoch became so close to God by talking to Him and obeying Him that one day God decided to take Enoch straight to heaven (Genesis 5:22–24)!

You don't ever have to be alone. Even when no one else is around, God is. He is ready to walk and talk with you wherever you go. If you take time to talk back and follow His direction, you'll be like Enoch, taking a walk through life with the Creator of the world at your side.

Prayer Pointer

Lord, please be my closest friend for all of my life.

Bigger Than Bullies

Two people are better than one. . . . If one
person falls, the other can help him up.

Ecclesiastes 4:9–10

Can you imagine what the people in Noah's day must have thought when Noah started building a gigantic boat in the middle of dry land? They must have made fun of him. And everybody probably told him he was crazy.

We know those folks weren't listening to God like Noah was. And in the end, their foolishness cost them their lives. Noah's story (Genesis 6–9) reminds us that being friends with God makes a lot more sense than listening to people who don't know Him.

What about you? Do you have any areas in your life right now where you are listening to the world instead of God? Consider the list below, and circle any areas where you might not be fully honoring God.

- Music choices
- TV shows/movies
- Friend choices
- The way you speak to parents
- The way you act at school
- The way you spend free time

Ask God to forgive you, and pray for strength to stand strong like Noah. Have a parent or trustworthy friend help you stay true to God by asking you each week how you are doing in the areas where you are struggling. By joining together with Christian friends in the fight against sin, you will stand even stronger.

Prayer Pointer

Father, help me love good and hate evil. Please
give me friends who will help me stand strong.

Fighting Friends

And God can give you more blessings than you need.

2 Corinthians 9:8

Jacob and Esau were twin brothers born to Isaac and Rebekah. You might think that since their story is found in the Bible, they were a happy family. But you'd be wrong! Jacob and Esau were total opposites, and they didn't respect each other. Jacob lied to their father and tricked Isaac into giving him Esau's inheritance. Furious, Esau wanted to kill Jacob (Genesis 27). So much for family togetherness.

These two brothers let greed, deceit, and anger almost separate them forever. But God showed them a better way. Over time, both realized that God was faithful to take care of their needs and they didn't have to fight each other to live well. When they understood God loved them and would take care of them, they both wanted to forgive the other and restore their relationship (Genesis 33).

Can you think of a friend or family member who has something you want but don't have? If so, tell God about it. Ask God to give it to you, too, if it will bring Him glory. But if God chooses not to give it to you, ask Him to make you content and thankful that He always provides everything you need. Now you can be happy for your friend and grateful that God has you covered too.

Prayer Pointer

Lord, help me not be greedy or selfish with
others. I trust You to take care of my needs.

Why Bother?

"THE second most important command is this: 'Love your neighbor as you love yourself.'"

Mark 12:31

Joseph was one stuck-up brother. At least, that's how his brothers saw it. Whenever he came around, he'd say something about a dream he had that showed he was better than them, and he was always wearing that colorful coat their dad gave him. It was nauseating! One day the brothers got so mad that they threw Joseph in a well. First they planned to kill him, but later they decided to sell him as a slave to Egypt. Either way, they thought they'd be rid of him for good!

Of course, that wasn't the end of Joseph's story. God stayed with him and blessed him in Egypt. Though Joseph went through many hard trials, God prepared him to be Egypt's leader who would save that part of the world (including his brothers and family) from starvation! (You can read the whole story in Genesis 37–45.)

Each one of us has people in our lives we wish weren't there. Whether it's their personality, their style of clothes, or their habits, there's something we just don't like, and we try to avoid them. Sometimes we even make fun of them. But Joseph's story reminds us that our God wants us to love everyone, not just the ones we click with. So instead of looking for a way to ditch the different kids or say things that are unkind about them, ask God to let you see them through His eyes. Everyone has unique qualities that make him or her special.

PRAYER POINTER

Lord, help me love others and see them like You do.

Give or Take

[Jesus] said, "It is moRe blessed
to give tHaN to Receive."

Acts 20:35

Delilah was beautiful, and Samson was incredibly strong. From the outside, they looked like a perfect match. But their hearts were very different. Samson served God, but Delilah served the Philistines, Samson's (and God's) enemies.

Eventually, Delilah tricked Samson into giving her the secret of his strength, which was his hair. Then she told that secret to his enemies, who cut Samson's hair, captured him, put out both of his eyes, and locked him up in prison. Samson made a very bad decision when he chose Delilah as a friend. But God was a true friend to Samson, and He allowed Samson's strength to return one last time to put an end to two thousand Philistines (Judges 16).

Building good friendships begins with finding others who serve God like you do. To keep friendships growing strong, you have to look for ways that you can encourage, support, and build up your friends. But if you discover that you only like them when they're doing what you want them to do, then you know you have stopped loving them God's way. And now, like Delilah, you are just using them. Instead, ask God to show you how you can better serve your friends. You'll all be happier in the end!

PRayeR PoiNteR

Lord, I don't want to use people to get my
way. Please help me love them well.

21

Queen of Heart

God will make you RICH iN eveRy way so that you can always give fReely. ANd youR giving thRougH us will cause maNy to give thaNks to God.

2 CoRiNthiaNs 9:11

Things were looking pretty grim for Esther. Her parents were killed, and she was Jewish and living in a country that didn't like the Jews. But her cousin Mordecai came to the rescue. He raised her as his own daughter and taught her the ways of God.

Then the king needed a new wife, and he ordered all the young women to come to court so he could pick a queen. Though many women were brought to the king, he chose Esther. She was crowned queen of Persia!

Surrounded by bodyguards and servants and all the luxuries of palace life, Esther could have easily forgotten about Mordecai and the other Jews. But she didn't. She ended up risking her very life to save Mordecai and the Jews from imminent death. (You can read the whole story in the book of Esther.)

When you are elected to a special club or make the team that your friend didn't, do you stay true to your friendships like Esther did? Esther's story reminds us that while God may grant us good things in life, those blessings are never meant to be used for selfish reasons. Good friends use their God-given gifts to love and serve others.

PRayeR PoiNteR

Lord, help me be humble when I succeed and look
for ways to honor You and bless others with it.

> You want me to be completely
> truthful. So teach me wisdom.
>
> Psalm 51:6

Job wasn't happy. In just a short amount of time, God allowed Satan to send a horrible storm to collapse the house where all Job's children had been celebrating. They all died. His crops were destroyed. His health fell to pieces. And Job's wife encouraged him to curse God and die.

But even in his misery, Job didn't curse God even though he wanted an explanation for the hard times God had allowed. Without holding back, Job cried out to God in tears, asking for understanding and relief.

And guess what? Even though God didn't answer his question, He talked to Job, and He comforted him in his sadness. God wasn't afraid of Job's questions. With power, holiness, and love, God helped Job to grow in trust and love of God. (Job's whole story is the book of Job.)

Do you have questions or frustrations about the way God runs His world? Have you had sad events in your life that you just don't understand? Don't bother hiding your feelings. Bring them to God, and talk to Him like Job did. You may not get all the answers you are looking for, but God will give you peace and comfort you with His love.

Prayer Pointer

God, thanks for handling my tough questions
and loving me in my confusion and hurt.

Status Cling

Brothers [and sisters], never become tired of doing good.

2 Thessalonians 3:13

Everyone expected Ruth to go back home. After all, she had family back in Moab, and her husband had just died. Naomi, her mother-in-law, told her it would make better sense if she left to find a new husband.

But Ruth wouldn't budge. Naomi had taught her about the God of Israel and had become like a mother to her. Ruth clung to Naomi and told her she would go with Naomi wherever she went.

God rewarded Ruth's loyalty by leading the two women to Naomi's relative, Boaz. Boaz eventually married Ruth, and they had a son who not only cheered up Naomi in her old years but who was also a part of Jesus' family line! (You can read all about Ruth and Naomi in the book of Ruth.)

Ruth's story shows us how rewarding it can be when we stay loyal to our friends, even when it's difficult. When our friends do things that make us mad, it's very tempting to give up and look for another friend somewhere else. But we need to have staying power like Ruth. Be willing to work through the problems with your friend, and trust God to take you and your friend where you need to go.

Prayer Pointer

Jesus, I want to be loyal like Ruth and like You. Please help me have staying power when times get tough.

Treasured

> "Your heart will be where your treasure is."
>
> Matthew 6:21

What's your favorite thing that you own? Is it an expensive doll or a new video game? A trampoline or a closet of clothes? List them in order below:

_____

Now imagine your best friend wanting that thing. Would you be willing to give your most prized possession away?

Jonathan was. He was best friends with David, the famous giant slayer. He wanted David to know he was really important to him. So Jonathan took off his robe, belt, armor, sword, and bow and presented them to David as gifts. Even though Jonathan loved being the prince who would one day be king, he was willing to give it all up to honor David because he loved him as much as he loved himself (1 Samuel 18:1–4).

What a beautiful picture Jonathan gives us of true friendship: to put others' needs in front of our own. Are you a good friend like Jonathan, willing to give up what you treasure in order to honor your friends? Or do you tend to hold back and serve yourself more? Ask God to give you a heart like Jonathan's, one that doesn't hold back from doing good for your friends.

Prayer Pointer

Jesus, thank You for giving up the treasure of heaven so that You could save me. Help me love others like Jonathan did and You still do.

The slap of a friend can be trusted to help you.

Proverbs 27:6

David had come a long way. From simple shepherd boy out in the fields to king of all of Israel, David had grown in size and power. Sadly, he let his selfish desires take his eyes off the God he loved, and instead he focused them on Bathsheba, a woman he wanted. Worst of all, she was already married to a good man, a soldier in David's army. Thinking he'd never get caught, David ordered Bathsheba's husband to be killed during battle. *Now I can have Bathsheba as my own wife*, David thought.

But Nathan, a man of God, came to David. Even though it was very risky, he let David know that God saw what David had done and was not pleased. David didn't argue or get mad at Nathan. Instead, he was glad Nathan was brave enough to tell the truth and help him repent, which he quickly did (2 Samuel 11–12).

Have you ever had a parent or friend tell you that you were doing something wrong? It's not easy to hear someone correct us, is it? Yet God uses our parents and caring friends to help guide us down a better path of obedience. We just have to learn to listen so that we can keep growing closer to God and to others around us.

Prayer Pointer

Lord, please help me listen to correction
and turn from doing wrong.

Talking Power

You are young, but . . . be an example to
show the believers how they should live.

1 Timothy 4:12

All alone in a strange place, in the house of her master, and without her mom and dad, a servant girl from Israel was faced with a choice. She could have stayed quiet. She could have done just the job expected of her and no more. But the brave little girl from Israel had some really important information that she knew could save the life of Naaman, her master. So she told Naaman's wife about Elisha, a godly man from Israel who could pray to God and possibly heal her husband from his leprosy, a deadly skin disease.

Even though she was very young, the servant girl convinced Naaman's wife to listen. In turn, the wife encouraged Naaman to contact Elisha. In the end, Naaman was healed, God was glorified, and a little girl showed what God could do through her bravery (2 Kings 5:1–14).

Naaman's story reminds us that we are never too young to trust God to do great things through us. Often, God gives us parents or teachers who will listen to our ideas and pray with us and for us. They become the friends we need in order to be brave and follow God, no matter what.

Prayer Pointer

Thank You, God, for those in charge of me.
Help me work with them to honor You.

Perfume and oils make you happy. And good advice from a friend is sweet.

Proverbs 27:9

Mary was excited, but she was also concerned. An angel had told her she was going to have God's baby, but she wasn't even married to Joseph yet. She knew the people in her village would probably say bad things about her. Yet she was still thrilled to be a part of God's plan to save His people.

But Mary didn't tough it out on her own. She went to live with her older cousin, Elizabeth, for several months. Elizabeth loved God, and she was also pregnant. God had given them each other for comfort and friendship as they trusted Him to work out His mysterious plan for their lives (Luke 1:26–56). What a blessing!

God doesn't want you to go through life all alone either. He made all of us to need one another. List below any parents, teachers, or friends who can encourage you to follow God:

_____

_____

If the list is shorter than you'd like, pray and ask God to help you find good friends who love God. Then make an effort to spend time building a good friendship with each person. Like Mary and Elizabeth, you can help each other stand strong in the faith!

Prayer Pointer

Lord, please help me find friends who can
support me in the tough times.

Starting Over

"Yes, if you forgive others for the things they do wrong, then your Father in heaven will also forgive you for the things you do wrong."

Matthew 6:14

As soon as the rooster crowed, Peter knew he had made a horrible choice. Instead of standing strong and supporting Jesus after the soldiers arrested Him, Peter acted like he didn't know Jesus. He instantly knew he had been a terrible friend and didn't deserve a second chance (Mark 14:66–72).

But that's not how Jesus saw it. After Jesus died and rose, He appeared to Peter and let him know that all was forgiven. Jesus wanted him to stay His friend and start following God's ways again (John 21:15–19).

Have you ever hurt your friends' feelings by doing something mean? Or have they done something wrong to you? Jesus reminds us how important it is to forgive ourselves and forgive others when they hurt us. Today, if you can think of a friendship that needs to be mended, don't wait another minute. Call your friend and work out the problem, and be sure to admit any wrongdoing on your part. Then ask for forgiveness or forgive your friend, and put the past behind you both.

Prayer Pointer

Father, thank You for forgiving all of my sins. Help me forgive others too.

Endless Devotion

In your lives you must think and act like Christ Jesus.

Philippians 2:5

Jesus knew what was about to happen. Soldiers would arrest Him. His closest friends would desert Him. And He would be crucified on a cross. You would think He would have spent His last night on earth as a free man doing whatever He wanted.

And He did! Jesus took off His robe, put on a servant's outfit, and washed His disciples' feet. Even in His last hour, Jesus wanted His friends to know how much He loved them and loved serving them. And He wanted them to do the same for others (John 13:1–17).

What are some ways you like to show your friends how much you love them? Write them down here:

_____

_____

Now pick one from your list, and look for a way today to show God's love to your friends.

Prayer Pointer

God, please help me find new ways to spread Your love to the world with creativity and selflessness.

Undivided Heart

> Teach me Your way, O Lord; I
> will walk in Your truth; unite my
> heart to fear Your name.
>
> Psalm 86:11 NKJV

Judas seemed to fit in with the others, didn't he? He traveled wherever Jesus went. He listened to the same sermons and saw the same miracles as the eleven other disciples. He was even in charge of handling the money people had given Jesus for ministry (John 13:29). So what went so tragically wrong?

Judas had a double heart. No, he didn't have two physical hearts! But his spiritual heart had two very different interests. Judas liked the idea of hanging out with an important person who might end up as Israel's king, but he didn't really believe what Jesus was saying about being God. He was in the friendship for what he could get out of it, not because he loved Jesus. So when the religious leaders offered Judas money to betray Jesus, Judas chose money (Matthew 26:14–15).

Judas gives us a pretty clear picture of what a fake friend looks like. And if we're not careful, we can be the same way toward God and our friends. If we only follow Jesus when it's easy, or if we only make friends with people who give us what we want, then we have double hearts like Judas. Divided hearts can never love like Jesus.

Prayer Pointer

Jesus, help me be true to You and my
friends. Give me an undivided heart.

God says, "Be quiet and
know that I am God."

Psalm 46:10

It was a big day! Jesus was coming to the home of Mary and Martha to have dinner and teach many people who were coming to hear what Jesus had to say. So Martha got her party game plan together. She knew just what was needed to make the day a success.

There was only one problem: Mary, her sister, wasn't helping. It was impossible to do all she had planned by herself. Totally mad, she went straight to Jesus and said, "Why don't You tell her to help me?" But Jesus saw something Martha didn't. Mary was happy sitting at Jesus' feet, soaking in all He had to say. Martha was so busy that she was missing the truly important thing: learning from Jesus. "Mary has chosen the right thing, and it will never be taken away from her," He answered gently (Luke 10:38–42).

Did you know that we are a lot like Martha most of the time? Whether it's running to games or recitals or school, we are constantly busy. Even church can be packed with activities. But how much of your loved ones do you miss because of the busyness? Ask yourself, "Do I just think about God, or even my friends, or do I actually talk to them and listen to them? Do I ever stop running around just to spend time with them?" Make an effort today to slow down and spend time with God and those you love.

Lord, I don't want to be distracted from what
is most important: You and Your people.
Help me spend my days wisely.

Extra Activity!

Record how you typically spend your day in each time block. When you are finished, check over your day. Are you spending too much time in one area?

6:00 a.m. – 8:00 a.m.: _____

8:00 a.m. – 10:00 a.m.: _____

10:00 a.m. – 12:00 p.m.: _____

12:00 p.m. – 2:00 p.m.: _____

2:00 p.m. – 4:00 p.m.: _____

4:00 p.m. – 6:00 p.m.: _____

8:00 p.m. – 10:00 p.m.: _____

SHOW RESPECT FOR all people. Love the
brothers and sisters of God's family.
Respect God. HONOR the king.

1 PeteR 2:17

D o you like to sew? Tabitha sure did! She loved to sew robes and other kinds of clothes to help the poor people in Joppa, the town where she lived. In fact, she was always looking for ways to help and serve other people, and she had become like family with the widows in the area because of her service.

But one day Tabitha got really sick and died. Her friends were *so* sad! Then they remembered that Peter was in town, so they sent some men to bring him to the house where they were keeping Tabitha's body. Peter came, and he prayed to Jesus for help. Then he told Tabitha to get up, and she did! God raised her from the dead! As a result, lots of people in Joppa started following Jesus (Acts 9:36–42).

And that's exactly how the members of God's family are supposed to work. Tabitha spent her days serving others and helping the poor. Then, when she was in desperate need, her friends helped her. And God was behind it all, helping everyone see what a powerful Savior He is. What can you do today to love and serve your family, friends, and neighbors around you?

PRayeR PointeR

Father, thank You for our family of believers.
Help me love and serve them well.

Speak Up

> Speak up for those who cannot speak for themselves. Defend the rights of all those who have nothing.
>
> Proverbs 31:8

Onesimus was in a bit of trouble. He had been a slave, but he ran away from the family he was serving. Then Onesimus met Paul, who shared the gospel with him. Onesimus repented of his sins and turned to Jesus as his Savior.

But now it was time for Onesimus to go back to the family he abandoned. Paul wanted him to return not only to mend the bad relationships, but also to share with the family all the good things God had taught him through Paul. But Paul didn't send Onesimus back empty-handed. He included a letter—what is now the book of Philemon—asking the family to receive Onesimus not as a slave, but as a fellow brother in Christ! Since the family members were also believers, Paul knew they would respond with open arms, taking Onesimus back as a loved child in God's family.

Paul knew that asking Onesimus to return to the family was a difficult request. So he helped him by speaking up for him. Do you speak up for your friends when they have a need? Whether it's asking a parent or teacher to help them or remembering to pray for them daily, good friends always stick up for one another and stay loyal to the end.

Prayer Pointer

Lord, help me remember to pray for my friends and get them the help they need.

Always be ready to answer
everyone who asks you to explain
about the hope you have.

1 Peter 3:15

They had listened to Paul preach about the gospel. They even had to flee from their home in Rome because of their Jewish heritage (Acts 18:2). But through all the training and trials, Priscilla and Aquila came to know God and His ways very well.

So when a man named Apollos began teaching in the synagogue about Jesus, Priscilla and Aquila listened closely. Even though Apollos was very educated, he did not know the full truth about who Jesus was and how He had come to save people. So Priscilla and Aquila met with him to teach him all about Jesus so he could preach the gospel in the right way (Acts 18:24–28).

Priscilla and Aquila were good friends to Apollos because they listened and told him the truth about Jesus. What about you? Do you have any friends who need to hear about Jesus? Have you ever asked them what they believe? Learn from Priscilla and Aquila. Be bold and brave, sharing what you know about Jesus so your friends can grow closer to God and work with you in sharing the Good News with the rest of the world!

Prayer Pointer

God, please help me study Your Word so I
know how to share truth with others.

Write It Out

All Scripture is given by God and is useful
for . . . teaching how to live right.

2 Timothy 3:16

Of all the Bible friends (or foes!) we learned about, which story stuck with you the most? Why do you think it made such an impact on you?

_____

_____

_____

_____

_____

_____

_____

_____

_____

_____

_____

_____

_____

_____

CRITTER CHAT

GROW IN THE GRACE AND KNOWLEDGE OF
OUR LORD AND SAVIOR JESUS CHRIST.

2 PETER 3:18

Have you ever heard of an axolotl? Also known as a Mexican salamander or a water dragon, these cute little creatures are amphibians that have lungs to breathe air and gills to breathe in water. They come in a variety of colors, but they start off small, looking a lot like a tadpole with arms, legs, and five-fingered hands and feet. But don't let their innocent look fool you. You have to keep axolotls separated from each other in the tank until they are six inches long. Why? Because they are cannibals. They think the other salamanders are food. But after they grow and learn to eat worms, they will no longer hunt each other and will actually enjoy being together.

Kids can be a lot like young axolotls. Some of them haven't learned how to be friends yet, so they may say or do mean things. Or they might seem selfish and hard to trust. But don't give up on people because of their mistakes. Instead, pray for them. Be kind, and give them time to grow. Then watch to see if God changes their hearts—and yours. You may be surprised over time to find that you become good friends!

PRAYER POINTER

Jesus, please help me be patient with myself and other Christians as we grow to become more like You.

Copy Cat

My child, listen to your father's teaching.
And do not forget your mother's advice.
Their teaching will beautify your life.

PROVERBS 1:8-9

Did you know that kittens aren't born knowing how to hunt? Even though they all look like pros when they're pouncing on some poor, unsuspecting chipmunk, the best hunters learned their skills from their mother. The mama cat trains her little ones how to stalk, catch, and kill their prey. Though the whole idea is a little gross, kittens need these skills so they can grow up strong and take care of themselves.

Fortunately, our mothers don't teach us how to stalk and kill creatures. But there are plenty of skills that we can learn from our parents. Even when it seems like parents are just making rules for no real reason, trust that they know what they are doing. Their life experience and time with God give them a better understanding of life situations and how to deal with them. So listen to what your parents have to say, and follow their example. By imitation and obedience, you will grow up strong in the Lord and be able to lead others on the same path of wisdom. And remember, your friends are in training under their own parents. Always show other parents the same respect you show your own. You never know when God will use them to teach you a new skill for life!

Prayer Pointer

Lord, thank You for guiding and training
me through my parents.

41

Each part of the body does its own work. And this makes the whole body grow and be strong with love.

Ephesians 4:16

When fall is coming, and as you are standing outside, you hear a familiar honk overhead. Just as you suspected, you see a large group of geese flying in a *V*-shaped formation as they journey to their new destination. But why do they fly in a *V*?

Geese know a little secret about teamwork. If a goose were to try to fly a long distance alone, it would get tired and have to stop for rest. But when geese travel together with the head goose at the point of the *V*, the trip is easier. The lead bird pushes against the wind, making the resistance against the geese following behind significantly less. Each goose flies slightly higher than the one in front of it to take full advantage of this phenomenon. When the lead goose gets tired, it falls back into the formation and another goose takes the lead. By taking turns in the front, the geese are able to rest easier, fly smarter, and keep going until they reach their destination.

Geese aren't the only ones who work better in groups. God created people to do better when they are working together. If you tried to build God's kingdom on earth all by yourself, how far do you think you would get? If you do your part and use the gifts God

has given you, and every other member in God's family on earth does the same, imagine the impact you all could have! Instead of growing tired in doing good, we would encourage each other and lend strength to one another until the work is done.

—————— Prayer Pointer ——————

Father, thank You for adopting me into Your family.
Help me work with others to stay strong in You.

Otter Delight

Trust the Lord and do good. Live in the land and enjoy its safety. Enjoy serving the Lord.

Psalm 37:3-4

Otters seem to love to play, and their sleek, long bodies are perfectly suited for it. Twirling and swirling in the water, they chase and swim with beauty and ease. They also seem to love to slide down riverbanks, turning travel into fun time too.

But otters aren't all play. They make time to eat, sleep, and groom. Without frequent grooming, otters would lose their oily coat that helps them glide and float in the water. All of their activities are equally important to help them stay healthy and fun little otters!

We like to play, too, don't we? Playing with your friends is a great way to build your friendships and knock off some stress. But just like otters, you also have to make time for the other important activities in life to stay well-rounded and healthy. Sleep restores your strength. Work at school and at home helps you learn needed skills for life. And grooming should become an important part of your life just like an otter. Nobody wants to hang out with someone who smells or doesn't take care of themselves. So scrub up, work hard, and play with all your might. And when your head hits the pillow at night, thank God for the gift of friends and a fun life.

Prayer Pointer

God, thanks for making life fun! Help me find the balance between play and everything else I need to do.

Camo Power

We know that in everything God works
for the good of those who love Him.

Romans 8:28

You can stare in the tank for several minutes without seeing a thing. Suddenly it looks like the sandy bottom is stirring. Is something swimming? Well, it wasn't really the bottom. It was a flounder, a very flat fish with both eyes on top, camouflaged perfectly in the sandy setting. God designed it to blend in so well that predators (and people, for that matter) can't see it, keeping it safe in an otherwise dangerous place.

It seems that God is really good at disguising things, including Himself. Sometimes we feel like God is nowhere around. It's easy to feel this way because we can't see Him with our eyes. We get worried when things go wrong and wonder sometimes if anybody even cares. Then God lets us see a ripple, like the camouflaged flounder on the move. It might look like a friend who called at just the right time to check on us. Or a hug from Mom. Or an act of kindness from your sibling. God is always present with us, even though we can't see Him, and He is always at work in our lives to strengthen and grow us.

Prayer Pointer

Lord, thank You for being with me,
even though I can't see You.

> Go watch the ants, you lazy person.
> Watch what they do and be wise.
>
> Proverbs 6:6

How would you like to have a conversation with an ant? Maybe you'd like to tell it that its friends shouldn't bite, or that it should build its colony somewhere else. Unfortunately, you don't have the special pheromones (body chemicals) that ants have, which allow them to communicate with each other. These unseen but very powerful chemicals help ants alert other ants to objects around them. Messages like "I've found food" or "Attack the intruder" can spread rapidly throughout the colony, and all the little individual ants can work together quickly and efficiently to conquer their goal.

Learning to communicate well is important for humans too. The way you look at your friend when you speak, the tone of your voice, and the words you say are all ways you communicate what you are thinking and feeling. If you want to be like the ants and learn how to pull people together for a common goal, you first have to put selfish thinking aside. You also have to stop trying to do everything by yourself. Talk to others in a way that lets them know you recognize their value. Be encouraging and positive, and listen to them when they respond. By learning from each other and supporting one another, your group of friends will grow stronger, as will your power to do good.

Prayer Pointer

Lord, thank You for using something as small
as an ant to show me a better way to live.

The LORD is my shepherd. I have
everything I need.

Psalm 23:1

Throughout the Bible, God often compares His people to sheep. And He tells us He is our Good Shepherd. But have you ever wondered why sheep need a shepherd?

Sheep have a, well, sheepish nature. They scare easily, and they tend to band together for protection. Left alone, sheep will follow one another, even though none of them knows where the flock needs to be going. They end up wandering aimlessly and become easy targets for predators such as wolves or wildcats.

Now can you see why God calls us the sheep of His pasture? As long as we are keeping our eyes on our Shepherd, we know where to go and what to do. And we know we are safe. But when we quit watching Him and start looking at all the people around us, copying their behavior and going where they go, we are in danger of getting lost. Our friends can be a strong support for us if they love God and are following Him too. Ask the Great Shepherd today to surround you with His flock—the people who listen to His voice—so that you can follow Him together.

Prayer Pointer

Jesus, thank You for leading and watching
over me. Help me keep my eyes on You!

Social Slowpokes

> People love and trust those
> who plan to do good.
>
> Proverbs 14:22

With long, gangly arms and full-body fur, sloths seem like they were made for giant hugs. And in a way they are—just not for people. They are uniquely designed to climb and hang from tree limbs, where they can slowly eat a meal of leaves. Of course, that's not all sloths do slowly. The digestion process from one meal of leaves can take over a *month*! They can sleep fifteen to twenty hours a day, which doesn't help with their friend making. Most sloths don't really socialize with other sloths, except for sometimes sharing the same branch.

If we want to become friends with someone and stay friends with that person, we can't just sit back like a sloth and hope things work out. Instead, we have to work at the relationship. What does "friendship work" look like? It looks like talking with and asking questions about the other person, listening well, and arranging times to hang out. If you wait around for the other person to do all the work, she might just leave you hanging—and that's only fun for a sloth! Ask God for His Spirit to help you care enough to reach out and respond well to all the people He puts in your path.

Prayer Pointer

Father, keep me from being lazy in my
relationship with You and my friends.

On the Hunt

Control yourselves and be careful! The devil is your enemy. And He goes around like a roaring lion looking for someone to eat.

1 Peter 5:8

Who's the king of the savanna? The lion, of course. Why? Because lions are pretty much the top of the food chain, if you don't count people. Ranging from 250 to 500 pounds, these massive cats aren't the fastest creatures on the plain, but they are rather sneaky. Lionesses (female lions) do most of the hunting and tend to work in groups. Since they lack speed, they surround a herd quietly, working hard to remain hidden. Then, when a weak or slow member of the herd breaks away from the group, the lionesses pounce and almost instantly kill their victim.

Did you know that God says Satan is like a roaring lion, looking for someone to kill? God wants you to know that you have an enemy who wants to destroy you, just like the lioness hunts to kill her prey. Using a strategy similar to the lions', Satan wants to separate you from the group—God's family—so that he can trick you with his lies. If you start listening to him and don't have anyone around you to tell you the truth, he can crush your faith. That's why it's so important to stay connected to God and His people at all times. We help each other stay safe in the truth.

Prayer Pointer

Lord, help me keep connected to You, and
protect me from Satan's schemes.

A Swimming Idea

Jesus has the power of God. His
power has given us everything we
need to live and to serve God.

2 Peter 1:3

Want to go for a swim? How about a two-thousand-mile-long one in a cold ocean? If you were an Alaskan salmon, you would think such a venture was normal, because it is for these spectacular fish. Salmon are born in a freshwater stream in Alaska after hatching from their moms' eggs. As they grow, they travel downstream until they reach the ocean at just the right time when their bodies have adapted to salt water. They spend anywhere from one to eight years swimming more than two thousand miles in the Pacific Ocean. Amazingly, they then find the stream they traveled down years ago and begin an incredibly difficult journey back upstream, jumping up waterfalls and escaping hungry bears and fishermen along the way. Once they finally reach their birthplace, the salmon lay eggs and let the new generation take over the process.

Watching a salmon swim upstream is both awesome and exhausting because of the work and determination required of the salmon. Yet God has gifted these creatures with the strength for the journey. You too might find that swimming upstream—swimming against the culture—is too hard. It might seem like wearing the same clothes, listening to the same music, and acting the same way as

the non-Christians around you would just be easier. But easier isn't always better. When we follow God, even when it's hard, He rewards us with unthinkable blessings. God's way always leads us to a greater purpose and new life.

Prayer Pointer

Jesus, please give me strength to fight the
world and follow Your way instead.

Defense Downer

"THe LORD is my Rock, my place of safety, my
Savior. My God is my Rock. I can Run to Him for
safety. He is my shield and my saving strength."

2 Samuel 22:2-3

Not surprising news flash: almost everyone is afraid of skunks. And who can blame us? Skunks have a reputation for a horribly foul-smelling spray they shoot straight from . . . yes, their rear ends. But actually, skunks are not aggressive animals. They usually give plenty of warning, like hissing or stamping or even doing handstands to let predators know they mean business. As a last resort, the skunk will spray, causing potential temporary blindness, vomiting, or illness in the predator—not to mention the stench that only gets worse when they try to wash it off.

People, like skunks, tend to defend themselves when they feel threatened. The result can be just as devastating as skunk spray. Have you ever had a close friend suddenly turn on you, calling you names or being mean? It is likely that you have scared or hurt her in some way, and she thinks she needs to defend herself. Or do you tend to lash out when your friends hurt your feelings? Jesus says that we need to let Him do the defending. Our job is to keep loving others and work out our problems through positive conversation. It works a lot better than skunk spray.

Prayer Pointer

Jesus, help me keep calm when others wrong
me, and give me wisdom to work it out.

Swan Song

THANK THE LORD because He is good.
His love continues foreveR.

1 CHRONicles 16:34

There are several birds known for loyalty, but none are as beautiful as the swan. Elegant white feathers and a long regal neck have earned these special birds a place of honor in royal courts, poems, and stories. Equally enchanting is the way swans relate to one another. Most swans choose a partner and stay with them for life. Even though they may fly to another place in colder weather, they always return and claim their place together.

Such loyalty is hard to find in the human world. Many friendships break apart because people lose interest in one another or they move on to find someone they think will be better. But God's love is forever, and He wants His people to love others the same way. Being a loyal friend means sticking with someone, even when times are hard or they are bothering you. But sometimes you can't help when friendships end. People move and lives change. Thankfully, technology is making it easier to stay connected. Ask God to help you be a good friend, even if your friends are far away, and to give you friends who will stick by your side no matter what comes. And ask God to help you stay loyal to Him all the days of your life

PRayeR PoiNteR

Father, thank You for always being my friend. Help
me be loyal to my family and friends too.

Soft Spot

"I will put a new way to think inside you. I will take out the stubborn heart. . . . And I will give you an obedient heart of flesh."

Ezekiel 36:26

H ave you ever seen an armadillo? It's pretty funny looking. Its back and shoulders are covered with a special type of bone and layers of tough skin that form a protective plate, but its underside is soft. To protect their softer side, these little creatures rely on their tough outer shell to protect them. Flexible bands of skin allow some species of armadillos to roll up into a complete ball to surround themselves with their armored skin. Others burrow into the ground to keep safe.

Some people seem to wear armor like armadillos. To protect themselves from getting hurt, they act mean or closed off to people who try to befriend them. If you come across kids who act really tough and are unwilling to let anyone be their friend, chances are they are trying to protect their feelings. These kids think if they shut others out, they will not get hurt. If someone you know is acting like an armadillo, don't give up trying to show them they are loved. God can use your encouragement to reach past their tough outside to help heal the hurts they feel inside.

Prayer Pointer

Lord, I don't need to shut others out with armor because You protect me. Help me love others who are too afraid to reach out.

Eagle Eye

"People look at the outside of a person,
but the LORD looks at the heart."

1 Samuel 16:7

How's your vision? If it's really good, your optometrist would probably say you have 20/20 vision, meaning you can see objects clearly from twenty feet away. But if the doctor said you had eagle eyes, you'd have to marvel at yourself. Eagles have 20/4 vision, meaning they can see something twenty feet away as clearly as they could if it were only four feet away. This unique ability enables them to spot small rodents and other prey scurrying on the ground, even when they are soaring hundreds of feet up in the air. Simply put, eagles see the world a lot more clearly than people can.

Since God made the eagle, can you imagine how strong God's vision is? His sight is so powerful, He can see inside us to our very souls. He sees your thoughts and motivations—and everyone else's too. So when it comes to making and keeping friends, we know that God has a better perspective on our situation than we do because He can see more than we can. So instead of blindly going into a friendship, ask God to help you see that person the way He does. Ask for wisdom so you can know if that friendship will honor God.

Prayer Pointer

Lord, I need You to help me see this world through Your eyes.
Please give me Your wisdom.

Tuned In

Human being, look with your eyes and
hear with your ears. And pay attention
to all that I will show you. That's why
you have been brought here.

Ezekiel 40:4

At dusk, you might just see a bat swooping down toward your head. Fortunately, before impact, the curious winged creature abandons course, only to dive at another seemingly invisible target. What is that bat doing? It's listening! And if it listens well enough, it gets to eat. Bats have a special sensory function called echolocation, which enables them to hear the sounds they make as those sounds echo off of distant objects. They use this information to determine how close or far away their flying insect meal might be. Once they've locked on a target, they dive with precision to capture the unsuspecting victim.

Even though people don't have the bat's remarkable ability, God has given us the ability to hear other people. No, we're not testing people out as potential meals. But God does want us to listen for the sound of other people's needs. If we are always talking or are busy doing other things, we'll miss it. We have to tune in and focus specifically on the person God has placed in our path.

As your friends speak to you, ask yourself:

- "What is my friend really trying to say?"
- "Is there any need she has that I can meet?"
- "How can I pray for her?"

As you learn to pay attention and listen to your friend's heart, you will gain a deeper understanding of her and become better equipped to love her like Jesus.

Prayer Pointer

Lord, help me tune in to the needs around
me so that I can better serve You.

A Howling Mess

I may speak in different languages of men or even angels. But if I do not have love, then I am only a noisy bell or a ringing cymbal.

1 Corinthians 13:1

At dawn or dusk, you can hear their screeching cries. Special features in their vocal chords allow howler monkeys to shriek so loudly that others more than three miles away can clearly hear their message. And what are howler monkeys trying to say? "Back off! This is our territory!" they're shouting to any other monkeys or predators that are getting too close.

While howler monkeys are fascinating to watch and hear, no one would want to listen to their screeching 24/7. And yet sometimes that's exactly what we humans do with one another. God says that when we talk or act without love, we sound like a noisy bell or a clanging cymbal. Complaining about our lives, our friends, or our situations has a similar effect. It sounds awful, and it drives other people away. That's why God tells us to make sure we soften our words and actions with the sound of thankfulness and love. If you find yourself complaining, remember the howler monkey, and close your mouth. Ask the Lord to fill you with the sweet and gentle words His Spirit brings. Then tell God and others how grateful you are for the blessings God has brought into your life.

Prayer Pointer

Lord, please make all of my words pleasing in Your ears.

Puppy Love

My God will use His wonderful riches in Christ Jesus to give you everything you need.

Philippians 4:19

Have you ever seen a mother dog give birth? Rarely does she have just one or two puppies. Most larger breeds can have anywhere from four to nine little ones, and they all wriggle and squirm around right after birth. Then miraculously, they move toward their mother's belly, where they each find a place to nuzzle and nurse, drinking their mother's life-giving milk.

God wants us to remember the miracle of puppy love in our own lives. Those little fur balls don't need to fight each other for food (though they may have to climb over and under to get a spot!). God provides for all the creatures in His creation, especially you. God brought you into this world with the purpose of protecting you, providing for you, and making you His own. You do not need to compete with your family or friends for the things you think you need. God is more than able to supply all the goodness you need in life. You just need to stay nuzzled up to Him.

Prayer Pointer

Jesus, You are all that I need. Forgive me for being selfish instead of sharing Your love with others.

You are my Hiding place. You
pRotect me fRom my tRoubles. You
fill me witH songs of salvation.

Psalm 32:7

on't take it personally when your pet box turtle hides its head. Some turtles can pull their arms and feet into their shell too. It's their natural way of protecting themselves when they think they are in danger. Once they feel safe again, turtles will stretch out their heads and limbs and begin exploring the world again.

Do you ever feel like pulling inside of your "shell" like a turtle because you feel shy or scared around others? Sometimes it feels safer to read a book or play on a phone or gaming device because we don't know if others will like us or we aren't sure how they will respond to us. But you don't have to withdraw like a turtle. You have your own protective layer: God. He loves you and thinks you're wonderful just the way you are. So you can walk with confidence into that room of people or carry on a conversation with a friend and truly speak your mind. God's love gives you the safety to come out of your shell and make friends with the people He has placed in your path.

PRayeR PointeR

Lord, You are my hiding place. Give me confidence
to talk and connect with others when I am afraid.

Duck Feathers

Love does not remember wrongs done against it.

1 Corinthians 13:5

Have you heard the saying "Don't worry about it. Just let it roll off your back"? It means to forget about the bad things that have happened and focus on the good instead. This saying is inspired by our feathered friends—birds! Unlike mammals, which have hair as protection, birds are covered with feathers. Feathers are uniquely constructed to shelter birds from wind and rain while also providing the lift they need to fly above their predators. To become water repellent, birds use their bills to spread the oil from a gland at the base of their tails to coat their feathers and give them water-resistant qualities. Then they can float on water, dive underneath water, and stand in a rainstorm without ever getting the soft, downy feathers underneath the outer layer wet.

In many ways, acting like a bird can help when developing friendships. Because your friends are imperfect just like you, there will be times when they say mean things. There will be times when they are selfish instead of serving or cruel instead of kind. Instead of dumping their friendship, remember the birds. Let your friends' actions roll off your back and into the forgiveness Jesus offers both them and you. Extend kindness and understanding, and you'll find your friendships will take full flight.

Prayer Pointer

Lord, help me not take other people's faults so seriously. Help me forgive like You forgive me.

Prickly Problems

Stop doing evil and do good. Look
for peace and work for it.

Psalm 34:14

D o you have friends or family members who tend to lose their temper quickly? It seems like you never know what you are going to say to set them off, and once they're angry, it's hard to settle them down. When you find yourself in a particularly prickly situation, remember the porcupine.

Porcupines look like overly large rodents (which they are) with bushy fur. But interspersed throughout their soft fur are sharp, pointy quills—sometimes as many as thirty thousand! When a porcupine is relaxed, so are its quills. But when it senses danger, the porcupine's body tenses, and the quills stand on end in protection. Predators who attempt a bite often leave with a face filled with quills that remain in the victim due to the barbed (think fishhook) shape at the tip. Porcupines grow new quills to replace the ones they lost, so they are always ready to defend themselves.

Now think about your hot-tempered friends. If you don't want them to prickle up, pray and seek God's help for a peaceful way to talk with them. Steer clear of topics you know are upsetting. Over time, they just might learn to trust you and be able to relax in your company, keeping their pointed "quills" flat at their side.

Prayer Pointer

Lord, help me be patient with others and look for
ways to keep conversations honoring to You.

So God made the wild animals, the
tame animals and all the small crawling
animals . . . God saw that this was good.

Genesis 1:25

t's amazing how we can connect God's creatures to our own
lives! Which animal describes your friendship style best?

_____

_____

_____

_____

_____

_____

_____

_____

_____

_____

_____

_____

_____

_____

FRIENDSHIP STARTERS

Phone Smart

I call to you, God, and you answer me.
Listen to me now. Hear what I say.

Psalm 17:6

Situation 1: Someone is calling, and it's not for you.

The phone is ringing. You check the caller ID, and you are pretty sure it isn't for you, so you are really tempted to ignore the call. Isn't that what voice mail is for?

No! People much prefer to speak with other living people, not recordings. Even though it may feel a little uncomfortable at first, here's what you can say when you answer the phone:

You: "Hello?"

Them: "Um, hi! This is _____. Is your mom home?"

You: (Choose from the following, depending on the situation)

a. "Yes, she is. Wait just a minute, please." (Then walk the phone to your mom. Don't yell for her to come!)

b. "I'm sorry, but she can't come to the phone right now. Would you like for me to leave her a message?" (This is when you grab a pencil and some paper.)

Situation 2: Your friend calls.

You: "Hi, _____ (say their name)."

Them: "Hi. What are you doing?"

You: "Nothing much. Just _____ (tell them whatever you've been doing lately). What about you? What's going on with you?"

Them: "I am hanging out in my room, listening to some music."

You: "Cool. Well, hey, you want to go do something this week, like _____ (name some options, like coming over to spend the night, going to a church event, movies, etc.)?"

Them: "Yeah! That'd be awesome. Let me ask my parents." (*Comes back.*) "They said I could on Friday. Does that work?"

You: "Let me check with my parents." (*Comes back.*) "They said it was fine! Come over at noon. See you then!"

Situation 3: You call a friend, just because!

You: "Hello! This is _____ (say your name). May I please speak to _____ (say your friend's name)?"

Them: "Sure, hold on just a minute. Let me go find her."

You: "Thanks!" (Wait quietly until you hear your friend's voice.)

Friend: "Hey, what's up?"

You: "Not much. Just calling to see what you're doing. How is _____?" (Be sure to ask her questions about things you know she likes or events that have recently happened to her. For instance, if she plays a sport, ask her how it's going. Or if she has been reading a book, ask her if she liked it. Just let her know you know what has been going on in her world and you are interested.)

─────── Prayer Pointer ───────

God, help me be mindful of others' feelings
in every conversation I have.

> WHEN you talk, you sHould always be
> kind and wise. THEN you will be able to
> ANSWER eveRyONE iN tHe way you sHould.
>
> Colossians 4:6

Everybody loves lunch, right? For some, it's a nice break from class to catch up with friends. But for others, it can be the most stressful part of the day. The "Who will I sit with?" and "What will I say?" questions can get you so uptight that they ruin your appetite. But no need. Just come prepared with these simple conversation tips, and lunchtime will go down easier than ice cream!

Unless your seat is assigned, it can be hard to know where to sit. If you're the first one there, stay toward the middle so that you'll have people on all sides to chat with.

If the kids sit in groups, try sitting with different groups each day. Then choose the one that best seems to match your interests. Once you've found some people you want to know better, follow these guidelines:

Do

- Say hi to the people around you, making sure to mention their names.
- Think of a question to ask that will make them have to answer, like "How's the food today?" or "Did anybody watch _____ last night?"

- Listen for their answer, and think about what they said. Ask another question about their answer that will get them to talk more (for example, "What did you think of how it ended? Wasn't it crazy?").
- Volunteer some information about yourself (such as, "I went shopping yesterday" or "I won my soccer game last night"). Wait to see if anyone asks you questions about it. If not, offer a few more details. Then change topics if no one seems interested.
- Keep the conversation clean and God-honoring.

Don't

- Talk with your mouth full.
- Gossip about other people.
- Look down at your plate, too afraid to make eye contact. Be brave!
- Keep talking about a topic no one else seems interested in.
- Talk over someone else.

Prayer Pointer

Lord, help me be bold when approaching new faces, and give me courage to make new friendships in tough places.

> May He give you what you want.
> May all your plans succeed.
>
> Psalm 20:4

So you wanna throw a party? Awesome! Get-togethers are a great way to start new friendships. Parties take lots of prep—and prayer! So take a look at these party to-dos and ask your mom or dad to help you get your fun in motion:

1. Decide how many people you want to invite.
2. If you can't invite everyone, then mail invitations to each person, and ask your friends not to say anything to others about it. Feelings can get hurt if you aren't really careful here!
3. Plan food.

   - How many people do you need to feed?
   - Do you want to serve finger foods or have a sit-down dinner? Do you want salty or sweet munchies, or both?
   - What do you want to drink?
   - When will you need to start cooking or order pizza?

4. Plan activities. For formal parties, you can have a theme and pick games and activities that match your theme. But for more casual get-togethers, just have a list of options that you can give to your guests, such as board games, movies, nail-painting, and outdoor adventures.

5. At the party, be a great host.

- Listen to what your guests want to do, not just what you want to do.
- Help those who seem shy or afraid to join in the fun.
- Talk to everyone at some point.
- Have fun!
- Thank each person for coming.
- And don't forget to clean up when the party's over!

Prayer Pointer

God, thank You for celebrations that allow me to get together with my friends. Please help me find ways to serve them and You better each day.

THE LORD said to Him, "WHo made man's mouth? . . . Now go! I will Help you speak. I will tell you wHat to say."

Exodus 4:11-12

If you could avoid talking to adults, you would. But sometimes you just can't. You find yourself seated next to a grown-up at the dinner table. Or maybe your friend's parent is driving you home ... alone. What on earth are you supposed to say? You couldn't possibly have anything in common with an adult, could you?

Actually, you'd be surprised! Remember, adults were once kids just like you, and they like lots of different things. So instead of shrinking into your seat, hoping they don't see you, sit up tall and start up a good conversation using these tips as a guide:

1. Start with something polite, such as, "How are you doing?" or "Thank you so much for taking me."
2. Ask them something about themselves, such as, "So, what do you do when you're not having to drive kids around?" or "This food is great. It reminds me of this place near my house. Have you ever eaten at _____ ?" or "What's your favorite kind of food?"
3. They will probably ask you a question in return. Don't give a yes or no answer. Instead, explain with more details. For example:

Them: "Do you have brothers and sisters?"
You: "Yes, (sir or ma'am), I have two older brothers and one younger sister. My older brothers are _____ (give information about their ages or schools) and my younger sister is _____ (give information about her)."

4. Turn their question around and ask it to them: "Do you have siblings or other family in town?"

Before you know it, dinner will be over or you'll have reached your destination, and you'll have made a new friend in the process!

PRAYER POINTER

Lord, please give me courage when I'm
nervous and the wisdom to connect well
with others, no matter what their age.

> "If anyone accepts children like these in my
> name, then He is also accepting me.
> And if He accepts me, then He is also
> accepting the One who sent me."
>
> Mark 9:37

Your mom has asked you to help her teach her kindergarten Sunday school class, babysit your aunt's little ones, or entertain her friend's kids while she visits with her friend. The thought of playing with small children makes you feel:

A. excited and energized.

B. nervous and full of dread.

If you picked *B*, don't worry! Even though some people seem to naturally know how to handle little people, you can learn a few tricks that will help you be the best babysitter in town. You might even find that it's fun for you.

- Get down on their level. Sit down with them when they come in the room so they can get a good look at you and you can talk to them eye to eye.
- Adjust your expectations. Little kids aren't going to talk to you like a kid your own age would. Speak in shorter sentences, and use simple phrases. For example, don't say, "Hey, you wanna go outside and kick the ball or something?" to a three-year-old. Instead, hold out a ball so the child can see it and say, "Want to play with a ball?"

- Don't play above their level. Now is not the time to show off how far you can throw. Roll a ball to them or gently toss it. Playing with small kids means doing things on their level, not yours.
- Try variety. Little kids have very short attention spans. They won't stay on one activity for long. Plan for several activities, such as coloring, snack time, reading them a book, watching a video, or building with blocks.
- As you play, ask them simple questions about what they are doing. For example, if you are building blocks, ask them, "Are you building a house?" Or if you are reading a book, you can stop in the middle of the story and ask, "What do you think is going to happen?"

By the end of your time, you will be their new best friend, and they will have helped you learn that little kids aren't so bad after all!

Prayer Pointer

God, please help me be a good example to little ones so they can know You better.

Food for Thought

> You prepare a meal for me in front of
> my enemies. You pour oil on my head.
> You give me more than I can hold.
>
> Psalm 23:5

Whether it's just your family gathering for dinner or a big dinner party with lots of extra guests, it takes more than just good food for a grand time together. You have to learn the art of exchange: exchanging food and fun conversation in a way that everyone gets a share. Follow these simple dinner table tips to make every gathering a success.

- Volunteer to set the table before the meal. Remember: place the fork on the left of the plate, and the knife goes on the right. And if you need a spoon, place it to the right of the knife.
- Wait a minute! Even though your stomach's growling, you've got to tame your urge to suck up food like a vacuum cleaner. Wait for:

  1. Everyone to get seated.
  2. The blessing to be said.
  3. The food to be passed to everyone at the table. Take what's nearest you, serve yourself, then pass to the left.

- Thank the person who cooked the meal.
- Talk to the person nearest you. Say, "How was your day? Anything interesting happen?" or "Did you hear about…?" and tell them a fact you heard or learned.

- Listen to what others are talking about. Do you have a question or story that goes along with their topic of conversation? If so, then share it when the other person stops talking.
- While others are talking, you can eat. But don't start talking with food still in your mouth.
- Pay attention to the people who are being quiet. What question can you ask them to get them talking? Here are some options:

    1. "You sure are being quiet. What's on your mind?"
    2. "I haven't heard from you today. How are things going for you?"
    3. "Tell me about your day. How'd you do on that test/project/sport you were worried about?"

Prayer Pointer

Lord, thank You so much for blessing me with good food and good family to share it with. Help me bless others as much as You have blessed me.

I go to bed and sleep in peace.
LORD, only you keep me safe.

Psalm 4:8

It's always fun to be with friends. But it's even more fun when the fun doesn't have to stop. Sleepovers are the perfect solution. Not only do they extend the party, but they also allow time for friendships to grow deeper and stronger if you manage the extra time well. Here are a few tips to help your slumber party score a hit with your friends . . . and your parents:

1. Ask your parents in advance for permission. Work with them to plan a good evening.
2. Invite girls whom you know like each other.
3. Schedule different activities for the evening like doing manicures and pedicures, cooking dinner, making s'mores, or swimming.
4. As it gets late, change to quieter activities like board games or watching a movie.
5. Make a place for everyone to sleep near one another.
6. Turn off the lights so that people can sleep.
7. In the morning, help your mom make a good pancake breakfast before your guests go home.
8. Thank everyone for coming!

Prayer Pointer

God, thank You for giving me such great friends to hang out with. Help everything we do together to honor You.

When you talk, do not say harmful things. But say what people need—words that will help others become stronger.

Ephesians 4:29

Sometimes navigating new social territory can be tough, but now you've got tools to help you along the way. Can you think of a time you mishandled a phone call or a conversation at church? How would you handle that differently now?

_____

_____

_____

_____

_____

_____

_____

_____

_____

_____

_____

_____

_____

_____

_____

FRIENDSHIP FIXERS

Lonely Looks

Turn to me and be kind to me. I am lonely and hurting.

Psalm 25:16

Scenario

It's not that she doesn't have *any* friends. Bella knows there are plenty of people at church and school that she could call to invite over. *But how come nobody ever invites me?* she thinks to herself. *Why do I always have to be the one to ask? It must mean that they don't really want to be with me.*

Meanwhile, two streets down from Bella, Hadley is lying on her bed, staring at the ceiling. *I am so lonely!* she realizes. *Nobody ever wants to hang out with me. I wonder what's wrong with me.*

Solution

Both Bella and Hadley have the same problem: they feel alone and sad. If you could appear in their rooms right now, how would you encourage them?

The truth is all people feel lonely sometimes. Because of Adam and Eve's sin in the garden of Eden, their relationships with God and each other became messed up. But God has fixed the brokenness through Jesus, His Son. Now we have perfect friendship with God and never have to feel alone, because Jesus is with us always, even though we can't see Him. Whenever we're feeling lonely, first we need to talk to Jesus about it and ask Him to help us know He

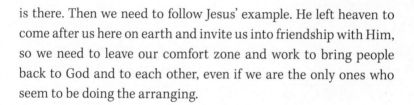

is there. Then we need to follow Jesus' example. He left heaven to come after us here on earth and invite us into friendship with Him, so we need to leave our comfort zone and work to bring people back to God and to each other, even if we are the only ones who seem to be doing the arranging.

Prayer Pointer

Lord, loneliness is difficult, but it reminds
me to talk to You and reach out to others.
Thank You for being a faithful friend.

> Do not change yourselves to be like the people of this world. But be changed within by a new way of thinking.

Romans 12:2

Scenario

Under normal circumstances, Emma is a relatively calm and respectful daughter. But her mother has noticed that something mysterious happens when her friends come over. Emma becomes very excited and giddy around her friends, and while her mom is glad she is having fun, she doesn't always like some of the behaviors she sees in Emma. In the excitement, Emma talks loudly over her family and guests. Her jokes and comments take teasing in a bad direction, often at the expense of her sisters, whom she normally enjoys. Worst of all, she argues when her mom asks her to do anything. What on earth is happening to sweet Emma?

Solution

Emma is trying to fit in with her friends. But somewhere along the way, she started to think her friends would be more impressed with her if she made fun of her sisters or proved that her mom is "not the boss of me." But do you think her actions will help or hurt her friendships? Why?

Everyone wants to fit in with their friends. It seems the older we grow, the stronger that desire to fit in becomes. But God warns

us not to start acting like the people who don't know Him. We don't need to be fake just to make people like us! God has made us to be an awesome blessing to our friends and family just the way we are. Emma, like the rest of us, needs to realize that she is a wonderful daughter of God who does not need to try to act cool or pretend to be something she isn't to be accepted. Instead, she can use her energy and humor to make people laugh, and she can love others the way God designed for her to do. And being able to bring people together . . . well, what's cooler than that?

Prayer Pointer

Lord, please help me be real with You and everyone else.

Be Happy with those who are Happy.
Be sad with those who are sad.

Romans 12:15

Scenario

It's Olivia's birthday, and everybody's ready to have some fun. Everyone except Skylar, that is. Skylar didn't get much sleep last night because her cousins slept over and were making too much noise, and now she is in a bad mood.

"Come on and join the fun!" her friends urge as Olivia waits to open her presents.

Skylar, though, sits sulking in her chair, no sign of a smile in sight. "Leave me alone," she answers. "I don't really want to."

Olivia frowns but tries to keep up the party spirit in spite of Skylar's bad attitude.

Solution

Who is Skylar thinking about in this scenario? What kind of effect does her bad attitude have on everyone else?

Though parties might not bring out your bad side, all girls feel the weight of mood swings at some point. Maybe your parents are enthusiastic about a new devotional to read to the family when you are feeling like being alone in your room. Or perhaps your friend is really sad about not making the team and needs to talk about it, and all you really want to do is run around and have some fun.

Sometimes our moods just don't match the situation at hand. What can we do?

Jesus says we should put others' needs before our own. We do not have to let our moods or emotions control our actions. Instead, we can decide to obey God and honor others. Even if we don't feel like it, we should participate or calm down or wait or talk or be quiet—whatever the situation demands. By matching our actions with the moment's needs, we can become a blessing rather than a bother.

Prayer Pointer

Jesus, please help me learn how to be
sensitive to the needs of others.

Be interested in the lives of others.

Philippians 2:4

Scenario

"Ugh! I'm so mad at her!" Libby complains to Abbey about their friend, Amanda, who was supposed to join them at the park today. "I mean, we have been planning to get together for weeks. And now, out of the blue, she says she has to stay home to babysit her little brother? Come on! That's just so rude."

"Well, maybe she has a good explanation that we just haven't heard yet," offers Abbey.

"I don't care. She just shouldn't do that," Libby snaps back.

Solution

Clearly, Amanda's decision to stay home changed Libby's plans, so her frustration is understandable. But perhaps Libby isn't seeing the whole picture here.

Maybe Amanda's family had a crisis come up requiring help, and Amanda was being unselfish and kind by giving up her fun day to watch her brother. But Libby could only see Amanda's actions as selfish because they hurt her plans. If Libby had taken the time to ask more questions or trust her friend's heart, maybe she could have seen the situation from Amanda's perspective. Looking at life from the other person's perspective helps us understand, love, and know better how to pray.

Prayer Pointer

Lord, help me see and love other people the way You do.

The Up Side

A happy heart is like good medicine. But
a broken spirit drains your strength.

Proverbs 17:22

Scenario

"Want to go fishing with me?" Erika asks her friend Taylor.

"No, I don't like to hook worms," Taylor responds.

"Okay, well, you want to go swimming, then?" Erika asks.

"I don't really like to get wet," Taylor answers.

Starting to get frustrated, Erika says, "How about a game of checkers?"

"No, I hate that game because I always lose."

At a loss for what to do, Erika gets up to leave. "Just let me know if you want to do something," she says with disappointment.

Solution

The problem with Taylor is that she doesn't seem willing to try any of the suggestions Erika made. She has a bad attitude about everything, and Erika isn't going to want to hang out with her anymore. If Taylor wants the friendship to work, she should make more of an effort to be with her friend. For example, she could say, "I don't like hooking worms, but I'll go to the lake with you," or "Sure, I can read by the pool while you swim." By staying positive, Taylor can keep the connection with her friend strong while they both find something to do together.

Prayer Pointer

Jesus, help me make my friendships
strong by keeping a good attitude.

CoNfess youR siNs to each otHeR
and pRay foR each otHeR. Do tHis
so tHat God caN Heal you.

James 5:16

ScenaRio

Kylee's eyes narrow as she watches her younger sister come into her room for what seems to be the billionth time. "What do I have to do to get it through to you?" Kylee's angry voice is rising. "All you ever do is bother me with all your nonstop talking! Get out of here!"

Kasey's large brown eyes well with tears as she turns around and closes the door behind her.

Solution

Kylee's hurtful words may have gotten her sister to leave, but at a terrible price of hurting their friendship and Kasey's feelings. If you ever find yourself in Kylee's situation, here are better actions you can take instead of to explode:

- Go ask Mom to help keep her out if you really need private time.
- Ask Kasey what she needs. If she just wants to play or talk, give her a ten-minute play/talk session, and then tell her you need your private time now.
- Take a minute to find a game or toy that can entertain Kasey for a while.

Whenever we blow it like Kylee did and lose our temper at someone else, we need to ask for forgiveness. In Kylee's case, it could sound like this:

Kylee: "Kasey, come here. I'm sorry I yelled at you like that. That was rude and mean. And I do like playing with you a lot of the time. I just needed some time by myself. Will you forgive me?"

Kasey: "Yes. I'm sorry I kept coming in your room."

Kylee: "Then we're friends again?"

Kasey: "Yep!"

Prayer Pointer

Father, help me be humble and ask for
forgiveness when I hurt others.

An evil person causes trouble. And a person who gossips ruins friendships.

Proverbs 16:28

Scenario

It's late, and the slumber party has quieted down. Now the girls are in their sleeping bags on the floor, talking into the darkness to one another.

"Hey, did you hear about Hannah?" a voice breaks in the quiet.

"Noooo, what are you talking about?" a girl answers from the corner.

"Well, I heard that she likes Ryan and tried to tell him, but he just laughed at her! I mean, how embarrassing is that!"

"Well, what was she thinking?" another girl pipes in. "He's really cute and popular, but she's . . . what can I say? Not."

Suddenly, all the girls are giggling, all except for Kaitlyn, one of Hannah's friends, who is listening to their conversation.

Solution

If you were Kaitlyn, what would you have done? Would you have joined in the giggling so you didn't stand out or stayed silent, hoping to hide in the darkness? Or would you have spoken up for your friend?

If the girls had been talking about you instead of your friend, you'd want somebody to stick up for you, right? But when people are talking about someone else, it seems different. In fact, the sin

is so sneaky and can feel so fun that it's easy to forget how much damage our words are causing. But God warns us to watch our words. When we gossip about others, when we relay hurtful information about someone else to other people, even if it is true, we have stopped honoring God. Instead, we are causing big problems in His family. Even staying quiet while our friends are gossiping isn't the right thing to do. You must be brave and remind each other that it's wrong to talk badly about others. When you do, everyone will see you are a trustworthy friend and maybe will even start following your example.

Prayer Pointer

Lord, keep my mouth from saying things I shouldn't.
Help me speak Your truth and love instead.

Be an example to show the believers how they should live. Show them with your words, with the way you live, with your love, with your faith, and with your pure life.

1 Timothy 4:12

Scenario

It wasn't that much of a problem when she was homeschooled, because she just didn't hear it. But now that Alli is in a public school, curse words seem as common as any other. In fact, taking God's name in vain and adding a couple of coarse words to every sentence actually seem like requirements if she wants to fit in with the cool kids.

It's in all the movies and TV shows and Internet sites my friends watch, she reasons to herself.

I guess it's just unavoidable, she decides.

I'm sure God will understand my situation, she rationalizes.

Solution

If you live in a home where bad language is commonplace or, like Alli, attend school or play a sport where everyone else says curse words without a second thought, then you know how easy it is to start talking like everyone else. But is Alli right? Does God not care what we say?

Actually, it's quite the opposite! God says His children are

to shine like bright stars in a dark universe. Many of the people around us don't know God, and they don't know what it means to follow Him. They are in the dark about what is good and true. By choosing our words wisely, avoiding gossip, and honoring God with what we say, we shine out God's purity and love.

Others will start to notice too. "Hey, why don't you curse?" or "Why are you always so positive all the time?" they'll say. And you will have a chance to tell them about how Jesus has given you an awesome life full of hope and love. Match the way you live with the words you say, and others will get a clear picture of what it looks like to belong to God.

Prayer Pointer

Lord, I want all my words to please You. Fill me with
Your love so that it overflows in what I say.

Walking Away

Try hard to live right and to have faith, love, and peace. Work for these things together with those . . . who trust in the Lord.

2 Timothy 2:22

Scenario

Emily was so excited to be invited to the sleepover. She is new in school and is trying to make friends. But during the party, the girls all decide they want to watch a scary movie. Emily knows her mom wouldn't approve, so she asks the girls to pick a different one.

"But we all love scary movies!" the host girl responds. "Plus, you don't even have to tell your mom."

Solution

Emily could cave to the peer pressure, but what would she get in return? She would be building friendships with girls who do not value what she does and hurting her relationships with her mom and God. Though it's hard to walk away, Emily would be wise to say, "Okay. Then I am going to go upstairs and read. Please let me know when it's over." Or even, "Well, I'm sorry. I guess I'll have to go home a little early. Thanks for inviting me."

In the process of finding good friends, sometimes we have to walk away from people who are not ready to follow God. We can pray for them and be kind to them, but our deep friendships need to form with others who love God too.

Prayer Pointer

God, give me wisdom to know when I
need to choose new friends.

Better than Blue Jeans

Religion that God accepts is this: caring
for orphans or widows who need help.

James 1:27

Scenario

Ari and her mom had worked hard on the yard sale, selling everything they no longer used. And it really paid off! They made a lot
more money than they had anticipated, even more than Ari needed
to buy those new, expensive jeans she wanted.

"What should we do with the leftover stuff and the extra money
we made?" her mom asks, curious to see what her daughter will say.

Solution

What would you say if you were in Ari's shoes?

It would be tempting to think about all the tops and shoes you
could buy to go with the new pair of jeans. But Ari has another idea.
She knows about a shelter for homeless women and children not
too far from their home.

"Do you think they'd want any of these leftover items?" she asks.

"Sure!" her mom answers. "They could use the stuff or sell it at
their thrift store."

That gives Ari another idea. "Do you think any of their kids need
new clothes? We could use the extra money to help them get some
new outfits too."

Prayer Pointer

Lord, help me remember the needs of
others and not just myself.

97

> Anger will not help you live a
> good life as God wants.
>
> James 1:20

Scenario

Ashlyn is with her family in the car. Her mom is up front, and her two brothers are on either side of her in the backseat. They are supposed to be headed for a vacation, but it doesn't sound like it.

"Andrew, stop touching me!" Ashlyn yells as she jerks her elbow away from her brother. A minute later she yells at her mom, "Why do you always listen to that music? You know I hate it. Turn it off!" Almost in the same breath, she rudely tells Kyle to give her the iPad so she can play her favorite game. And everyone knows Ashlyn won't be happy until she gets it.

Solution

Sounds pretty terrible, doesn't it? But that's the common noise of anger and self-centeredness. It jars everyone's ears and adds a bitter taste in their mouths. In this scenario, Ashlyn's outbursts are ruining the trip for everybody. So what is her problem? It's a sin area we all have: selfishness. And when other people block our goal of getting what we want, we often explode in anger. We have learned that people will give up and give in to our demands if we get angry enough. But that's not what Jesus taught us. He told us to consider other people as more important than ourselves and to

put others first. If Ashlyn had chosen to tame her anger and obey Jesus instead, the conversation would have sounded closer to this:

"Hey, Andrew, would you mind scooting over a bit? It's feeling a little cramped in here."

And, "Mom, when your song is over, may I listen to one of my favorites?"

And finally, "Kyle, I know you just got the iPad, but I'd also like to have something to do. Can I have a turn in, like, thirty minutes or something?"

—— Prayer Pointer ——

Lord, forgive my selfishness. Give me
Your patience and love instead.

Jilting Jealousy

"All people will know that you are my
followers if you love each other."

JOHN 13:35

Scenario

Avery and Julia have been best friends for as long as Avery can remember. But ever since the new girl, Alyssa, showed up, everything seems ruined!

"Did you really have to invite Alyssa to spend the night with us? Now she thinks she's a part of our group, and she follows us around at school too!" Avery accuses Julia.

"But I thought you liked her," Julia answers, confused.

"She's nice, but I don't want her stealing your friendship away from me!" Avery snaps back, frustrated.

Julia thinks for a moment and puts her arm around Avery. "We will always be best friends. But can't we be friends with other people too?"

Avery feels comforted a little, but the worry isn't all gone.

Solution

Making room for new friends when you already have good ones can be tricky. It's easy to stay comfortable with what you already know and love. But Jesus showed us by His example that He was always welcoming new people to be a part of His group, God's family. There was always room for more. While it may be natural to

feel jealous when you see your friend reaching out to others, you need to fight those jealous feelings with God's truth. Remember that God didn't give us strong friendships so that we could shut out the rest of the world. In fact, good friendships give us strength and courage to befriend others and share God's love, knowing that no matter what happens, our good friends will always be there to support and encourage us. God says other people will know we belong to Him when we love one another that way.

Prayer Pointer

Father, help me be open to new people and
friends to help grow Your kingdom.

Keep me from looking at worthless things. Let me live by your word.

Psalm 119:37

Scenario

Ashley heard the sound at the door but was too caught up in her game to notice who it was. Ever since she got the latest video game, she just can't seem to tear herself away from the screen.

Later, when her family loads into the car to go out to eat, Ashley is still riveted to her console.

"Honestly, Ash," her mom sighs. "Even when you're with us, it doesn't seem like you're really here. Can you put that thing away?"

Solution

Ashley has forgotten that real people are a lot more important than the games she is playing, and she is hurting her relationships by ignoring those around her. Here are some ideas that would help Ashley find some needed balance:

- Always make eye contact and speak to people when they first come in the room.
- If you have guests over, put the electronics away.
- Never bring a phone or game to the dinner table.
- Set a timer when you do play so you know when it's time to move on to something else.

Prayer Pointer

Lord, thank You for technology. Please help me honor You with my use of it.

Keep the Peace

"THOSE WHO WORK TO BRING PEACE ARE HAPPY."

MATTHEW 5:9

Scenario

Jade is fed up with Jackie. Jackie had promised to keep her secret, but she forgot and told it to some of her other friends anyway. Now Jade won't speak to Jackie. Meanwhile, Maddie, who is best friends with both Jade and Jackie, feels caught in the middle. If she sides with Jade, Jackie will get mad at her. But if she hangs out with Jackie, then Jade will feel betrayed. What should Maddie do?

Solution

God has called each of His kids to be peacemakers. But in tricky situations like this one, it can be hard to do. Maddie should first pray and ask God to help her friends stop being angry and be willing to forgive. Then Maddie could talk to Jackie about the problem she caused by telling Jade's secret. It could sound like this:

Maddie: "You know you shouldn't have told Jade's secret, right?"

Jackie: "Yeah, I know. I really didn't mean to. But now she's being a jerk about it all."

Maddie: "Why don't you just apologize? I hate to see you two fighting like this, and it makes life hard on me too."

If Jackie listens, then Maddie will have helped mend a friendship and honored God in the process.

Prayer Pointer

Lord, give me patience and wisdom
to be a good peacemaker.

Brave Face

> "Be strong and brave. Don't be afraid
> of them. Don't be frightened. The
> LORD your God will go with you. He
> will not leave you or forget you."
>
> Deuteronomy 31:6

Scenario

"Mom, I don't want to go in there!" Hayley moans.

"Honey, your dad and I are going to our Sunday school class, and it's not for kids," her mom says. "You have your own class, and I'm sure it will be fun."

"No, it won't," Hayley argues. "I don't know any of those kids in there, and they already have their friends. I'm just going to be left out."

"Well, you don't really have a choice. I'll come back to get you in an hour."

Hayley then enters the class, staring at the floor, and takes a seat off by herself.

Solution

Do you think the Sunday school class is as bad as Hayley predicts? What would you encourage her to do differently?

Have you ever had to be the new person in a group? Maybe you've moved to a new place and started at a new school. Or you've joined a new team or are living in a new neighborhood. Change

can be difficult, and walking into a place with new faces can be really scary. But you are not alone! God, your best Friend, is with you wherever you go. And He always has a way of connecting His kids with the friends they need. You just have to be brave and trust that God isn't going to abandon you. Instead, He has hidden treasures in the people around you that He eagerly wants you to discover. By hoping for the best and trusting that God has put you in this situation on purpose, you can be sure that God is working something really good in your life as you reach out to new people with His love.

Prayer Pointer

Lord, fill me with bravery as I face the challenge of making new friends.

Gifted

> THose paRts of tHe body tHat seem to
> be weakeR aRe Really veRy impoRtant.
>
> 1 CoRintHians 12:22

ScenaRio

Jasmine has dazzled the teacher with her answer once again. Lizzy grumbles quietly to herself, "She is such the teacher's pet," and she folds her arms.

In P.E., Jasmine is showing her friends some new tricks she learned at gymnastics. While everyone else seems impressed, Lizzy just grows angrier. *I bet I can do more push-ups than she can, though,* she thinks.

When she gets home, Lizzy tells her mom how annoying Jasmine is. "I think she's just showing off all the time!" she complains.

But her mom answers, "It sounds like Jasmine is a pretty special girl. But you know what? God has made you special too. You don't have to compete with Jasmine. You can both enjoy the gifts God has given each of you."

Solution

Jasmine's mom is right. God has given gifts to each one of His kids that are to be used for building up His kingdom. The problem is that we, like Lizzy's classmates, get stuck noticing flashy gifts and forget that the "behind-the-scenes" gifts like wisdom or kindness are equally important. God does not want us to look at other people and wish that we had the looks or personality or skills they have.

God made each one of us on purpose and for a very specific reason that often only He knows. We just have to trust Him that He knows what's best for us and thank Him for making us the way He did. Instead of being jealous of others or complaining about what we think we don't have, we need to start thanking God for every little thing about us. We are God's unique masterpiece! Ask Him to use your special design to bring Him the most glory, and He will be happy to do just that!

Prayer Pointer

Father, forgive me for comparing myself to others.
Thank You for making me like You did, and please
use my gifts to show Your glory, not mine.

Thanks a Lot

Give thanks whatever happens.

1 Thessalonians 5:18

Scenario

Brooke was so excited. Her mom had taken her to a painting class where she learned to work with oil paints. She decided to paint a picture for her friend, Brantley. She worked hard on it each week in class. After a month, she was finished. Once it was dry, she wrapped it up, eager to give it to her friend. But when Brantley opened it, she looked confused.

"What is that?" Brantley asks.

"It's a picture I painted for you," Brooke answers.

"Huh," Brantley grunts. "That looks kinda . . . messy."

Brooke tries hard to hide her disappointment.

Solution

Does it even matter what the picture looked like? Brantley missed the whole point of her friend working hard to give her something. Maybe that's why God talks so much about thanking Him and all the people He has placed in our lives. When we show gratitude, we reveal that we have noticed the good around us. Not only have we noticed the gift, but also the kindness of the giver. Just like Brantley, we all need to grow in gratitude, learn to recognize the blessings all around, and give lots of thanks to God and others who really need to hear it.

Prayer Pointer

Thank You, Jesus, for who You are and all You
do for me. Help me grow a grateful heart.

CReate iN me a puRe HeaRt, God.
Make my spiRit Right agaiN.

Psalm 51:10

There were some pretty helpful tips in this section, huh? Which one of these areas are you going to work on in your own life?

_____

_____

_____

_____

_____

_____

_____

_____

_____

_____

_____

_____

_____

_____

_____

_____

109

FRIENDS AT HOME

God gives the lonely a home.
Psalm 68:6

When you think of the word *family*, what words come to mind?

_____

_____

How would you describe your family?

_____

_____

Have you ever considered that your family was planned on purpose by God? It's true! Your parents or caretakers, sisters and/or brothers, were all uniquely created by God, just like you were, and put together to help each other grow closer to Him.

Sometimes it's hard to see the blessing, though. Parents can seem too strict. Siblings can get on our nerves. Life at home can feel crazy and unsettled. And suddenly God's gift to us might not look so good. But trust God's goodness. Believe that He has given you parents and leaders to guide and help you. Those things that bother you about your parents or siblings will actually help build your character if you handle them with prayer and obedience to God. Take time right now to thank God for your special family. And look for ways to share God's love with those He's placed around you.

Prayer Pointer

Lord, thank You for my family. Help me
learn from them and love them well.

On a Role

We are many, but in Christ we are all one body. Each one is a part of that body. And each part belongs to all the other parts.

Romans 12:5

Look at your car. How well would it move if the tires were flat? What if the steering wheel was missing? Or the lights didn't work? A car only functions well if all the parts are there and doing their job. If something goes missing or breaks, the whole thing suffers.

The same goes for your family. God designed families to function a certain way in order to roll through the ups and downs of life together. Husbands and wives are to love and respect each other, and children are to respect and obey their parents. We are all to be fueled by God's Spirit, allowing our lives to be driven by His guiding hand.

You have an important role in your family. You can be an encourager to your parents and siblings by the way you serve them. Speak the truth, but do it in love. Seek peace. Willingly follow your parents' direction. And pray at all times that God will keep you and your family finely tuned to His Spirit. Through prayer, obedience, and service, you are a powerful and important force of God's goodness, working in your family and in the world for God's glory.

Prayer Pointer

Lord, thank You for my family. Help me do my part in supporting and encouraging others.

> "Then the King will answer, 'I tell you the truth. Anything you did for any of my people here, you also did for me.'"

Matthew 25:40

D o you have a sister? If so, is she older? Younger? Fashion conscious or tomboy? Bold or shy? Do you have a similar personality, or are you as different as day and night?

No matter what the age or style difference may be, sisters can be a total delight if you learn how to treat them right. But—and this is the tricky part—you have to learn to lose in order to win a lasting friendship.

To build a beautiful friendship with your sister, here's what you need to give up:

- The right to always be right. Instead of arguing to win, work hard to listen and love.
- The right to your things. Whether it's a game, an outfit, or your favorite food, let her have the first pick.
- The right to win. Competing for attention always backfires. Believe it or not, you don't always have to be the best or the smartest or the prettiest all the time. You can also look for ways to encourage and compliment your sister on all the gifts God has given her.
- The right to privacy. Allow your sister to feel at home in your room and in your company. Invite her to share

what's on her heart without fear of your telling on her or
judging her.
- The right to be served. Follow Jesus' example, and seek
to serve her whenever possible.

Here's what you'll win:

- A closer walk with God
- Habits that help with all friendships
- A friend for life
- Probably access to her clothes too!

What can you do today to start a better friendship with your
sister?

Prayer Pointer

Jesus, thank You for my sister. Please give us a
lifelong friendship with each other and You.

We, Not Me

> Make me very happy by having the
> same thoughts, sharing the same love,
> and having one mind and purpose.
>
> Philippians 2:2

What do the following scenarios have in common?

- My parents have planned a family outing, but I want to spend the day with my friends. I argue until my parents give in.
- My mom asked us to clean up the living room. I'm trying to finish my game, so I keep playing, even though everyone else has started to pick up.
- During worship at my church, everyone stands to sing together except me. I'd rather sit and play with the bulletin.

If you guessed "selfish thinking," then you're right! In each of these cases, this girl is thinking only about her own needs and not the needs of the family around her or what God wants from her. But God didn't create us to care only for ourselves. Instead, God placed each of us in families, and God placed our families in the larger group of God's big family of believers.

Like a great coach, God instructs all of His people to work together as a team, worshipping, serving, and living a life filled with His love. Why? Because there's no better way for the world to see God's love than to see God's family loving and caring for each other.

Prayer Pointer

Lord, help me fight my selfish ways and
think like a team member instead.

CHildReN, obey youR paReNts tHe way tHe
LoRd waNts. THis is tHe Right tHiNg to do.

EpHesiaNs 6:1

Home might be the most challenging place to improve your friendships, but God put you in your family for a reason. How can you be a more helpful daughter? How about a better sister?

QUIZZING THE NIGHT AWAY

Winner Gives All

"It is moRe blessed to give tHan to Receive."
Acts 20:35

Jesus shows us that one of the best ways to be a friend is to give up your rights to serve others. But living selflessly isn't easy. Take this quiz to test whether you tend to be a taker or a giver.

1. Your mom just brought home a bag of candy from the store. You:

   a. Take some candy for yourself and hide the rest so the others won't find it.
   b. Go tell all your brothers and sisters so you can all share the fun.

2. It's time for everyone to get in the car, but there are a lot of people to fit in. You:

   a. Rush to get into the best seat and make others crawl over you to get situated.
   b. Volunteer to sit in the back so others won't have to crawl over.

3. You are starting to feel alone and wish you had someone to play with. You:

   a. Get angry at your friends for not thinking of you and inviting you over.
   b. Pick up the phone and ask your friends to come over for a visit.

4. You are listening to music in the car, but your brother wants to hear something else. You:

    a. Say, "Too bad. I was listening to this first."

    b. Say, "Okay, why don't we take turns listening to music we like?" and turn the station.

Survey Says

Giver: If you answered *B* to these questions, you are growing a servant's heart like Jesus.

Taker: If you answered *A* to any of the above, ask yourself whom it is you are serving in that scenario. Then ask God to give you a servant's heart like His Son's.

Prayer Pointer

Lord, please help me to see and serve
the world with a servant's heart.

We will speak the truth with love.
We will grow up in every way to be
like Christ, who is the head.

Ephesians 4:15

We know it's not right to lie. But telling the truth isn't always easy, especially when we know the truth might hurt the person with whom we are speaking. Harder still is learning to tell the truth with God's love. Check out these scenarios, and see how you rank at truth-telling God's way, with love and humility.

1. Your friend's zipper is down. You:

   a. Pretend like nothing's wrong.
   b. Start laughing uncontrollably and pointing.
   c. Whisper the embarrassing fact in her ear.

2. The teacher is writing on the board, and you notice that she misspelled a word. You:

   a. Blurt out to the class that she can't spell.
   b. Laugh with your friends about her mistake.
   c. Raise your hand and go up to her to tell her about the error.

3. Your best friend forgot your birthday. You:

   a. Give her the silent treatment for a whole week.
   b. Tell all your other friends how awful she is.
   c. Wait until she is alone and admit that her forgetting really hurt your feelings.

4. You met a new girl at the park who doesn't think Jesus is real. You:

   a. Get really angry and tell her she's stupid for not believing in Jesus.
   b. Get scared of her and stop playing with her altogether.
   c. Calmly and lovingly explain why you believe that Jesus is God's Son and continue to treat her with kindness and respect.

If you answered *C* for all of the above, then congratulations! You have learned the secret to sharing truth with the love and peace God wants. If you chose some other options, think of reasons why that route misses God's heart of love for the other person. Then pray and ask God to help you always tell the truth in love, just like how God speaks to you in His Word.

— Prayer Pointer —

Jesus, You were never afraid to tell the truth in love. Help me be like You.

Buddy Building

> So comfoRt each otheR and give each otheR
> stRength, just as you aRe doing now.
>
> 1 Thessalonians 5:11

Jesus says that good friends build each other up and help each other grow stronger. But encouraging other people doesn't always come naturally, especially when we don't feel very good about ourselves or when we find ourselves competing with our friends instead of supporting them. So how big of a friend-builder are you? Take this quiz to test your buddy-building strength.

1. Your friend just made a bad grade on a test that you aced. You:

   a. Pretend like you don't know her score.
   b. Laugh and tell her that you didn't even have to study.
   c. Give her a hug and tell her you're sorry. Then ask her if she'd like to study with you next time.

2. If your friend hadn't missed the last catch, your team would have won the game. You:

   a. Throw down your glove and walk off alone.
   b. Walk up to her and tell her she should try a different sport.
   c. Smile and tell her, "Don't worry about it! We all make mistakes sometimes."

3. Your friend just got exactly the kind of puppy you've always wanted. You:

    a. Act like you don't care.

    b. Tell her how much trouble it is to have a pet dog.

    c. Tell her how excited you are for her and ask if you can come over to see it.

4. Your sister has just spent the last hour getting ready for a dance. You look at her and say:

    a. "I think that outfit makes you look fat."

    b. "Why are you wearing your hair like that?"

    c. "You sure look pretty. I hope you have fun!"

If you picked *C* for your answers, then you are a trained buddy-builder! But if you answered *A* or *B* for any of the above, you could use a little strength training. Remember that your words can bring joy or despair to the person who hears them. Choose them carefully, asking God to help you find creative ways to let your friends know they are loved, special, and safe in your supportive friendship.

Prayer Pointer

Jesus, give me words of encouragement
so I can build up my friends.

I know what you do. I know about your love, your faith, your service, and your patience. I know that you are doing more now than you did at first.

Revelation 2:19

You know a good friend when you find one, but what exactly are those qualities that make a good friend so great? Look at the list below, and circle the traits you hope to find in your friends. Put a check mark beside the ones you see in yourself.

- ☐ **Kind**: answers gently and sees the bright spots in others
- ☐ **Loud**: takes control of conversations or simply talks loudly so others will listen
- ☐ **Shy**: afraid to say what she really thinks
- ☐ **Encouraging**: knows how to make others feel good about themselves
- ☐ **Brave**: willing to try new things and venture outside of her comfort zone
- ☐ **Curious**: asks lots of questions to find out more details about others
- ☐ **Hot-tempered**: reacts to small things and gets angry easily
- ☐ **Godly**: loves Jesus and isn't afraid to talk about Him with others
- ☐ **Servant-hearted**: seems to look for the needs around her and works to meet them

- ☐ **Sarcastic**: uses biting comments to get a laugh or feel important
- ☐ **Wise**: looks at people and situations from an understanding perspective
- ☐ **Insecure**: seems to need others to tell her she is good at things
- ☐ **Bossy**: always tells other people what to do and how to do things

Now take a look at the list. Which of these character traits best describe you? Underline the traits you'd like to change, and ask God for help to do it. Can you think of any other character qualities you'd like to see in yourself or others? If so, list them here:

_____

_____

_____

_____

_____

_____

_____

Prayer Pointer

Lord, please fill me with Your Spirit so that I
can be the kind of friend I need to be.

FRIENDSHIP FUN ZONE

Friendly Fruit

D o you want to be the best friend ever? God says good hearts always start with Him. When we let His Spirit rule our lives, we produce fruit—spiritual fruit—that gives others a taste of just how sweet Jesus is. Find all the different kinds of fruit of God's Spirit in the word search below.

Love

Joy

Peace

Patience

Kindness

Goodness

Faithfulness

Gentleness

Self-control

S	G	K	I	X	F	N	G	S	U	A	Y
E	P	U	Y	J	N	I	Y	S	Y	G	M
L	E	X	Y	O	J	A	H	E	E	A	U
F	A	I	T	H	F	U	L	N	E	S	S
C	C	G	L	E	P	O	T	D	C	L	X
O	E	J	Z	G	V	L	J	N	O	H	Z
N	L	C	S	E	E	A	S	I	C	K	B
T	M	O	Z	N	Q	A	J	K	I	L	H
R	Q	T	E	E	C	N	E	I	T	A	P
O	U	S	G	O	O	D	N	E	S	S	P
L	S	B	Q	Z	V	W	V	O	S	T	Z
D	J	B	K	X	E	M	S	I	W	R	O

Built for Blessing

ecause we have God's Spirit living inside us, we have everything we need to build strong friendships and honor God in the
process. But we have to do more than just know the truth. We
have to apply it to our lives and work hard to live it out.

Search for the following words from 2 Peter 1:5–8 that describe
the qualities we must seek to add to our lives as we live for God.

Faith

Goodness

Knowledge

Self-control

Perseverance

Service

Kindness

Love

```
L  W  K  A  Z  F  D  U  E  E  S  E
W  O  Q  I  A  H  Z  Z  G  T  E  C
T  Q  R  I  N  E  D  D  W  T  R  N
T  Z  T  T  Y  D  E  V  O  L  V  A
Y  H  D  Z  N  L  S  N  W  I  R
Q  L  J  Q  W  O  Y  E  B  C  C  E
S  B  V  O  R  Q  C  O  S  Y  E  V
A  A  N  O  Q  X  S  F  O  S  L  E
G  K  I  Z  U  P  O  N  L  N  S  S
N  F  F  O  K  G  F  Q  H  E  P  R
G  F  N  H  H  F  S  O  H  B  S  E
G  O  O  D  N  E  S  S  V  N  T  P
```

Dressed for Battle

id you know you're a soldier in a great big war? Satan, our unseen enemy, has evil forces all around the world working tirelessly to tear God's people apart. If we don't watch out for Satan, we will fall prey to his tactics and fail to experience the victory that already belongs to us because of what Jesus did on the cross. God reminds us that the Spirit inside us is a lot stronger than Satan's evil forces. We just need to put on the armor of God listed in Ephesians 6 and keep our eyes focused on our army's Captain: Jesus Christ! On the next page, draw the pieces of the armor of God we need to put on ourselves each day.

Belt of truth

Breastplate of righteousness

Shoes of Good News

Shield of faith

Helmet of salvation

Sword of the Spirit